T0128912

Navigating the STORM

7 Truths to Mastering Our Lives

Beth Fortman-Brand
Matthew Schonbrun
Agnes Deason

BALBOA.
PRESS

A DIVISION OF HAY HOUSE

Copyright © 2017 Beth Fortman-Brand, Matthew Schonbrun, Agnes Deason.

All rights reserved. No part of this book may be used or reproduced by any means, graphic, electronic, or mechanical, including photocopying, recording, taping or by any information storage retrieval system without the written permission of the author except in the case of brief quotations embodied in critical articles and reviews.

Cover Painting and Illustrations done by Beth Fortman-Brand.

Balboa Press books may be ordered through booksellers or by contacting:

Balboa Press
A Division of Hay House
1663 Liberty Drive
Bloomington, IN 47403
www.balboapress.com
1 (877) 407-4847

Because of the dynamic nature of the Internet, any web addresses or links contained in this book may have changed since publication and may no longer be valid. The views expressed in this work are solely those of the author and do not necessarily reflect the views of the publisher, and the publisher hereby disclaims any responsibility for them.

The author of this book does not dispense medical advice or prescribe the use of any technique as a form of treatment for physical, emotional, or medical problems without the advice of a physician, either directly or indirectly. The intent of the author is only to offer information of a general nature to help you in your quest for emotional and spiritual well-being. In the event you use any of the information in this book for yourself, which is your constitutional right, the author and the publisher assume no responsibility for your actions.

Print information available on the last page.

ISBN: 978-1-5043-7793-5 (sc)
ISBN: 978-1-5043-7794-2 (hc)
ISBN: 978-1-5043-7823-9 (e)

Library of Congress Control Number: 2017905040

Balboa Press rev. date: 06/08/2017

Acknowledgments

Beth Fortman-Brand's
Acknowledgments

Tremendous thanks and appreciation go to my coauthors, Matthew Schonbrun and Agnes Deason, because without their total commitment of time, energy, and brain power, this book would not have been possible.

Next, I want to acknowledge my mother, Dr. Zita Fortman. Thank you for being an unconditional, loving mother; a lifelong friend; and my first marvelous teacher and for running our financial business successfully. We are grateful and appreciative of all your energy and input in critiquing and editing this book.

My deepest appreciation goes to my wonderful husband, Doug Brand. You have taught me to let go and just breathe. Without your adorable humor, consistent support, tremendous generosity, unconditional love, and continuing willingness to learn and grow with me, I would not be who I am today.

A special thanks to my first husband, Troy Stevenson, for teaching me that with great courage, love conquers all. Thank you also for your loving energy and input in editing and your insightful contribution to the back of this book.

Much gratitude and love to my dear friends Claire Candy Hough and Peter Hough for their unwavering encouragement and guidance with all aspects of this book. Thank you for strongly suggesting I do the illustrations and for your help with how to do it successfully.

Matthew Schonbrun's Acknowledgments

First and foremost, I want to thank my ema, Michele Paley, and my dad, Len Blonder, whose love, support, wisdom, guidance, openness, and non-judgment have allowed me the space and freedom to grow into the person I am becoming. Through all of my spiritual meanderings, you have never passed judgment upon me, nor have you wavered in your love of me. You held the space to allow me the room to expand and grow. What a tremendous honor it has been to be able to call you Mom and Dad!

I want to thank my dad, Harvey Schonbrun, and stepmom, Cherie Schonbrun, for their love and support and for always recognizing in me my greatest potential. You both have been great teachers to me, even though distance often limits the amount of time we get to spend with each other.

My deepest appreciation goes to my wife, Jacky Schonbrun. You have always allowed me to walk my path next to you, and I appreciate that you're always holding my hand on the journey. I love your openness, honesty, courage, and spirit; I truly would not be the person I am today if you were not in my life.

I'd like to thank my son, Liam Jacob Schonbrun, and my daughter, Skye Helena Schonbrun. Although you are still young at the time of this writing, I have learned so much from you both. I am starting to realize that I learn as much from you as you learn from me. You two are quite advanced beings, and I am lucky you chose me to be your dad.

I am deeply grateful to my sister, Bree Bandy. We have shared a unique journey together, and you have never wavered in your support and love of me. You are truly one of the most amazing human beings I have ever had the pleasure of knowing. I am honored you are my sister, and I am deeply grateful for your presence in my life.

A special thanks to Marco Aiello. You are my best friend, my mentor, and my family. You have taught me many spiritual truths along my journey, and watching you on your own spiritual journey is an honor. You are truly a master.

I'd like to acknowledge my first spiritual teacher, Pam Castillo. You introduced me to Neuro-linguistic programming, Reiki, energy work, and much more. I have no doubt we fulfilled a sacred contract entered into long, long ago, and I am grateful. It is true that when the student is ready, the teacher appears.

Finally, I'd like to express my deepest gratitude and thanks to my coauthors, Beth Fortman-Brand and Agnes Deason. What an incredible adventure it has been creating this book with you both. Not only would this work never have come into existence without you both, but in finishing it, we fulfill purposes set forth long, long ago. I love you!

Agnes Deason's Acknowledgments

I am deeply grateful to so many people who contributed their time and love to this book. Their influence is on every page. Thank you to my mother, Agnes Olsen and father, Jack Olsen who have been the core foundation in my understanding of unconditional love. Thank you to my understanding husband, who loves me beyond measure, for his soft wisdom and support. Thanks especially to Beth Fortman-Brand, with my total gratitude, appreciation, and love, as this book springs from your amazing insight, and to Matthew Schonbrun for your brilliance and ability to put ideas into words. Finally, with great love and devotion, I thank my friends and family—I could never adequately describe how much you mean to me.

Acknowledgments From
All Three Authors

Many thanks to Maia Berens, Evie Serventi, and Troy Stevenson for your wise and generous endorsements for the back of this book.

Although there are three authors, the full range of knowledge and skills necessary to write and publish a book like this successfully takes many others. Thank you to all who have contributed their valuable time, loving energy, and incredible wisdom to this book: Zita Fortman, Troy Stevenson, Claudia Brodie, Evie Serventi, Grant Pirie, Claire Candy Hough, Peter Hough, Michele Paley, Maia Berens, Paula Lawless, Martha Smith, Alex/Debra Hall, Rhoda Brand, Lori Cohen, Haviv Nissan, Bree Bandy, and Marco Aiello. Thank you. Much love, appreciation and gratitude to you all!

Introduction

The information contained within this fable comes from our desire to engage with and attempt to answer many of life's most challenging questions. This work centers on seven core truths that we have uncovered on our respective spiritual journeys. In attempting to make sense of the world we live in and by examining the joys and sorrows of our own personal experiences, we endeavor to find meaning in the purpose of life. We offer the information contained within to you, the reader, with an open heart.

The three of us, in our seeking, have incorporated only information and answers that resonate deeply within us and that we feel and know to be true. Our suggestion to you is to accept only that which resonates within you. Each and every one of us alive at this time is traveling his or her own journey, and each journey has the potential for many truths. We realize that each person's journey, whether it is cloaked in light or shadow, eventually leads to the same core truth of oneness. There are many paths one may take to get to that realization. No path is any better than any other. We wrote this fable in accordance with our desire to be of service to others who, like us, are seeking answers. We hope you receive it in the spirit in which it is being offered—with love, gratitude, and service.

The goal of *Navigating the Storm: Seven Truths to Mastering Our Lives* is to assist in shifting from a life lived in fear and limitation to a life filled with love and abundance. We realize that although this is a metaphorical story, the information is multilayered. Like a puzzle, as each puzzle piece fits together to form a complete picture, so too will these truths fit together to form a complete picture. If one's goal is to become adept at consciously creating one's life, then understanding the way in which our universe operates is essential.

Our universe is purposefully orchestrated to highlight two opposing forces: light and dark. These forces form the nature of a dualistic system that creates opportunities for our own evolution. This dualistic system is comprised of both loving and unloving experiences. In some instances, many of us are able to grow from painful experiences if we are willing to learn from them. One's perspective is important, and these seven truths might provide a foundation that will allow you to interpret experiences from a different perspective. Our intention is that you continue to work with each truth presented within these pages and integrate the knowledge into your daily life. Our hope is that working with these truths will result in more joy, love, and peace reflected in your everyday experiences.

We designed this story to elevate an individual into a state of awareness. Our intended purpose is to assist others in remembering the truth of our magnificence. This process occurs by becoming self-realized. We must embrace the self-realization that we create our reality not only through our thoughts, words, and actions but also in conjunction with the more expansive aspects of ourselves.

In this story, we have chosen to use caterpillars and butterflies to depict humanity because of the unique way a caterpillar goes within and transforms into a butterfly. The caterpillar is a metaphor for the part of us that is human, and the butterfly symbolizes our ability to embody our higher expanded selves.

Through the characters, we are able to see the multifaceted parts of ourselves, the complexities of life's challenges, and the impact we allow our experiences to have on our ability to love.

Spark represents the part of us that is an optimist seeking balance and driven to make known the unknown.

Omni represents our ability to access an unlimited awareness of how the universe is designed and operates from a place of universal love. Thus, Omni represents the higher expanded self.

Dawny represents the part of us that is hypnotized by the media yet has the potential to snap out of it with ease and is open to change.

Dusky represents the part in us that has no self-awareness and feels disconnected from emotional feelings. Dusky is a pessimist addicted to gossip and drama and unwilling to take responsibility for one's actions.

Gruff represents the part of us that feels lonely and isolated. Gruff operates from fear and holds the belief that the world is constantly conspiring against him. As a result, Gruff strikes first, rejects intimacy, and repels others.

The story represents a personal journey of self-discovery, self-worth, and self-love by remembering the truth of who we are and why we are here.

The Seven Truths

I.   If you always go within, you will never go without. Abundance is within.

II. Separateness is an illusion, we are never alone.

III. We are eternal and are all one.

IV. Thinking with our hearts and feeling with our heads allows for balance.

V.   You create your reality; your outer world is a reflection of your inner world.

VI. Love is the blueprint of creation; fear blocks our authentic power.

VII. Duality provides the opportunity to grow, and expressing gratitude enhances that growth.

1

*O*nce upon a time, in a grand place named Greenleaf, there lived a lovely, bright redheaded caterpillar named Spark. She still lived with her mom and dad, along with her three sisters and four brothers—it was a big family. Spark was the oldest, and as the oldest, she took on much of the responsibility of helping to raise her younger siblings.

Her parents were often busy providing food, shelter, and other things needed for the family's survival.

Spark didn't mind helping, because Spark and her family were close. She enjoyed playing teacher. Her students were her brothers and sisters and their friends. She was continually nurturing others and felt maternal. However, as she got older and her siblings were able to fend for themselves, Spark found herself with more and more quiet time and room to enjoy her own interests.

Spark loved taking long walks and exploring while admiring the beauty and tranquility of her surroundings. She felt connected to nature and was also aware of and sensitive to her environment and others. One of Spark's special relationships was with her grandmother, who lived nearby. Spark's grandmother was insightful, kind, and filled with wisdom that she loved to share. Spark was always inquisitive.

She enjoyed learning and being a student. As a result, Spark was never afraid to ask her grandmother questions about how things worked and why they worked that way. Her grandmother explained the importance of spending time alone and being comfortable in quiet contemplation. Spark spent many afternoons with Grandmother, chatting about great topics, such as the meaning of life and their true purpose in the world, and attempting to make known the unknown.

One afternoon, when she and her grandmother got together, Spark began to cry.

Grandmother said, "What is wrong, my love?"

Spark became angry while she continued crying. "I can't believe my sister. I know she's the baby in the family, but she isn't a baby anymore, and she makes me feel so angry!"

Grandmother said, "I am sorry you are upset. Why don't you come over here, sit next to me, and share with me what happened?"

Grandmother motioned to her and opened her arms up to hug her. Spark went over to her grandmother and fell into her comforting arms, and they hugged. Spark began to calm down and stopped crying. She sat up, took a deep breath, and said, "All I did was walk over to her while she was having a conversation with her friend, and I guess it was pretty heated. Actually, you know, when I think back on it, I realize she was already really upset. You know that since she was born, I have always helped to take care of her, so of course I asked, 'Is there something I can do to help?' You would think I had insulted her. Instantly, she turned to me in a fit of anger and yelled, 'It is none of your business! You are always trying to mother me! You are not my mother! Go away!' Well, that really angered me because I have been nothing but good to her. All her life, I have always been there for her, and now she speaks to me that way! I just don't understand. I didn't do anything wrong!"

Spark became visibly angrier and more upset as she talked about it.

Grandmother said, "I am sorry you are so upset. I am curious, though—how did you respond next?"

Spark said, "Not so great. I was just so shocked by it. I reacted with just as much anger. I said in a loud, harsh voice, 'Then don't ever ask me for help again!' And then I stormed off."

Grandmother said, "Ah, honey, I can see you are angry, but do you understand why?"

Spark became a bit annoyed at her grandmother's question. "Yes, of course—because she disrespected me!"

"So she hurt you?"

Spark, now a bit calmer, thought about how she felt. She recalled other situations in which she'd felt hurt by someone who had spoken angrily to her.

Spark said, "Well, I guess that's why. Okay, you are right. I am absolutely hurt. I have a right to be! I would never speak to her that way."

Grandmother said, "It may help you if you try to look at it from a different perspective. If you think about it, she was already in pain and very upset when you approached her. Now, if that's true, wouldn't that mean that her anger wasn't about you at all?"

Spark felt as if her feelings were not being fully understood and was still a bit confused and a bit annoyed at her grandmother for her line of questioning. "No, because it was me she was speaking that way to. So isn't it about me?"

"Well, not exactly, sweetheart, and I am sorry you are getting upset again. I promise I am not trying to minimize your feelings at all; my only desire is to help you understand something that happens to many of us in many situations. Sometimes we take our anger out on others even when it has nothing to do with them. What's incredibly important to understand is that we often misdirect our angry feelings.

"However, you can choose how you allow the situation to affect you. That's why, when you are dealing with others, it is extremely imperative not to assume anything and not to take things personally. Because there are always many obvious and hidden factors that contribute to how a person behaves. For instance, when you first saw your sister, she was already angry, wasn't she?"

"Yes." *Spark began to calm down again.*

"So if she was already angry, then can't you see that maybe her anger had nothing to do with you?"

"Kind of. I guess so," *Spark said.* "But why did she turn it on me?"

Grandmother said, "I have a little story that may help you better understand what I am saying. Years ago, the farmers would keep the packs of coyotes from harming their sheep by shooting the coyotes in the rear end with a salt-pellet gun. A coyote would feel the impact from the pellet gun and think the coyote next to him had bitten him, so he would in turn bite the coyote next to him. In reality, it was really the farmer who caused the pain. The coyotes weren't aware of the true cause of their pain and simply lashed out at the closest thing to them.

"In your situation, your sister was already hurt and in pain. You mentioned she was upset, and when you walked up to her and offered to help, she turned and took it out on you. Like the coyote next to the other coyote, you got bit."

Spark continued to feel better but still did not totally understand. "That makes sense now when you say it is not personal. But then how is it not about me if I felt the bite?" *Spark was still a bit confused about what to do with her pain.*

Grandmother, as usual, was patient and understanding. Grandmother knew that this was a wonderful teaching moment for Spark to learn not to always be reactive and at the mercy of others' moods and actions.

"What's not about you is her anger, that's what's not personal. I'm not at all discounting that you are hurt and you feel like she bit you. What I am saying is that the only part of this that is about you *is how you allow the bite to affect you and how you react to the bite. Fortunately, no one can make us feel anger or any other feelings. How we feel is up to us and has to do with what we are telling ourselves about the circumstances. You don't want to diminish your personal power by blaming others for how you feel. We all have the power to choose to control how we allow ourselves to respond to any situation. Spark, you can choose not to react by learning to stop and observe yourself before you react."*

Spark, looking bewildered, asked, "Huh? How does one do that—observe oneself?"

Her grandmother smiled with delight at her inquisitiveness. "If you want to learn to observe yourself, why don't you try this? Spend the next few days noticing your thoughts. After a time, you might begin to notice repetitious patterns of thinking; you might find

yourself having thoughts that are critical or judgmental. You can give those thoughts names, such as the judge, the critic, or the victim."

Spark said, "I guess I am willing to do that, because I really don't like feeling bad when others spew their anger at me, especially when I haven't done anything. Yeah, it's worth it. Okay, I am going to give it a go."

They hugged.

Spark said, "I love you so much, Grandmother, and I'm sorry I got a bit upset. You know that I always appreciate your insight."

Spark left with a strong sense of curiosity about what was going to happen when she did as her grandmother had suggested.

Over the next few days, Spark was surprised how many of her thoughts came from fear. She had always seen herself as a positive person.

A few days later, Spark and her grandmother met up. Both smiled, hugged, and sat on a big rock under a shady low-hanging leaf.

Grandmother asked, "Are you doing well? Were you able to observe your thoughts and come up with a name for your mind chatter?"

Spark smiled and shook her head. "As I think about it now, it's kind of funny and even pitiful that I am actually worried about what I observed. Because what I noticed is that I worry a lot. And now I am worried about the fact that I worry so much."

Grandmother said, "Really, sweetie? What about?"

"Well, like, will there be enough food? What if one of my brothers or sisters gets hurt or sick? What's gonna happen when Mom and Dad get old? How much longer will you be here, Grandma? Worrisome thoughts like those."

Grandmother said, "Wow, I had no idea you had all those worries."

"The strange thing is, I didn't realize it either until these past couple days, when I started observing my thoughts. So that's why the name I have decided to give the chatter in my head is the worrier."

Grandmother said, "That's perfect. You know, Spark, unfortunately, most of us tend to worry. It's wonderful that you are willing to make such an effort to grow. It is our ability to notice our chatter and name it that gives us the opportunity to start observing our thoughts."

Spark said, *"Got it! Observing our thoughts is the key to not being defensive or letting others offend you, like I did with my sister."*

Grandmother said, *"Exactly. Choosing to be the observer provides us the space and time to allow ourselves not to react. And being aware of what we are telling ourselves allows us to have control over how we feel. As we become the observer of our thoughts, we can begin to realize how our emotions are directly related to our thinking. Spark, the truth is, your conflict with your sister is an opportunity for you."*

Spark was puzzled. *"An opportunity for what?"*

"The opportunity to grow and feel more in control of your life. When we are willing to recognize that we are reacting or being defensive, we can learn to step back and observe before we react. The real benefit comes from not allowing the outer world to have such a strong influence on our emotional well-being. Not only that, Spark,

but once we can quiet the chatter and become an observer, we can access greater wisdom from within."

Spark smiled and said, partly joking yet being honest, "Greater wisdom from within? I thought wisdom came from people with experience and from reading books."

Grandmother smiled and chuckled a little. "You're not the only one who probably thinks that, but knowledge comes from many places. When we learn to switch to the position of the observer and not just react based on the chatter in our heads, we then can consciously connect to our inner source of wisdom. Our wisdom comes from our spirit, and it is always connected to us and is the part of us that is not physical. Our spirit is also sometimes called our higher expanded self."

Spark looked a bit baffled. "Wow, that's a bit much to grasp. Before we get any deeper, I want to get clear here, because I am very interested and really want to learn why I am not supposed to worry and the benefits of not worrying."

Grandmother said, "Oh, there are many benefits to stopping yourself from worrying, but I'll name just a few. First, when we project worry into the future, it blocks our ability to experience the present moment. That's because we are not able to be present to what is happening now if we are thinking about something else. Second, our thoughts are very powerful, as they are what determines how we respond or act toward an issue and can therefore influence our behavior. Third, where we focus our attention and how we feel about things influence our lives in many ways. For example, stress from worry releases chemicals in our body that can create illness. Also, we attract what we believe about ourselves and the world around us.

Unfortunately, worrying can ultimately contribute to an undesired outcome."

Spark looked visibly surprised. "Wow, I didn't realize the impact worrying has on my life! Oh no," she said, half joking, "I hope I don't start worrying about worrying now. All joking aside, how do I stop worrying?"

Grandmother said, "First, you do exactly what you have been doing the past few days. You learn to stop worrying by becoming the observer of your thoughts. This brings you into the present moment. Then, when you are in the present moment, you are able to make wiser decisions. In the present moment, your thoughts are more likely to represent the truth and not something that may or may not happen or that is out of your control. Also, Spark, one of the things you can do is ask yourself questions. For instance, 'Do my thoughts best

serve my well-being?' and 'Is my worrying going to help or change the outcome in a positive way?'"

Spark said, "Sounds like it's important for me to pay close attention to what I'm thinking so that I can begin to have a sense of control over my own well-being instead of letting others affect the way I feel."

Grandmother said, "Yes, and in addition to not being affected by others, observing your thoughts is a wonderful tool that gives you a sense of empowerment in all matters in your life."

Spark felt optimistic and was excited to use her new tools. They heard her brother calling her for dinner, and before she ran off, they hugged.

Spark said, "Thank you for your love and wisdom. I am looking forward to the next opportunity to observe myself and not react."

Since she was young, Spark had loved educating others. Spark was so excited about this new revelation she had learned that she wanted everyone in her community to know about it. Spark made it a point to share her new knowledge with as many as possible. However, not everyone understood or was ready to hear her message, because some were not as open as she was to new and different ideas. This resulted in Spark being shunned for being different and having strange and unconventional thoughts.

When her grandmother became aware of the situation, she approached Spark.

Grandmother said, "I have heard from your siblings that some people in the community are treating you unkindly. I am sorry for that. Sounds like your excitement to share what you learned didn't work out so well. I understand your generous nature and desire to share what you have learned; however, I have learned over my many years that people are more receptive when you lead by example. This allows them the space to come to you when the time is right for them. I think it is never wise to push or force information or knowledge onto others."

Spark nodded in agreement because she could relate to what her grandmother was saying, since she also never liked it when someone told her how she should think, feel, or act. "That's true."

Grandmother said, "We are all a work in progress, and you meant well, so don't be hard on yourself. Learn from it instead."

Spark and Grandmother kissed and hugged and then went their separate ways for their day.

As time went on, Spark's process of observing life, asking questions, and seeking answers provided her with the knowledge and awareness that things happened for a reason. She also learned that paying attention to her emotions was the first step in self-awareness and the key to staying balanced. She recognized these internal feelings as signals of higher wisdom that she could always trust. Ultimately, she learned to be guided by her gut feelings. By becoming the observer of her thoughts, Spark realized she was much more than just her repetitious thoughts. This realization brought her a greater sense of peace and strength.

Eventually, through trial and error, Spark developed a powerfully effective tool to create mindfulness for herself, and she used it all the time. First, she stopped and took a deep breath, because she was aware that focusing on the breath brought one into the present moment and allowed one to be mindful. That created the space to look within. Then she'd ask herself, "What am I afraid of?" and she was willing to listen to the small voice of her higher expanded self to achieve greater perspective. Over time and through leading by example, Spark became a respected leader within her community.

Recently, the weather patterns in Greenleaf had been changing. As Spark and her family found themselves struggling through increasingly cold, wet winters and harsh, dry summers in their search to find food, there remained great joy, appreciation, and profound love within the family.

On a not-so-typical morning, Spark awoke with the feeling that something wasn't right. As the day progressed, the weather changed drastically. The winds blew with ferocity that had rarely been seen before. The howling sounds were deafening as they pierced the usual quiet calm. Spark and her family moved quickly to find shelter from the wind, and they huddled close together under a large branch near the coastline. Suddenly, the ocean began to roar as the sea started to rise, causing twenty-foot waves to pound the shoreline. In an instant, a huge wave swept Spark away, as if she were a leaf being blown off a branch. She clung desperately to anything she could grab on to, but unfortunately, she was pulled away from her family and swept out to sea.

As the enormous wave carried Spark farther away from her family, she was smashed violently upon a rock jetty. Spark, disoriented and half conscious, frantically clung to anything she could find. She managed to feel some twigs underneath her, and she held on to them for dear life. Still clinging to the twigs, Spark felt a wave toss her high into the air, and before she felt the impact upon landing, she blacked out.

Chapter 1 Highlights

**It's important to make time for self-reflection.

**How you choose to handle a situation is about you. However, when you are dealing with others, it is important not to assume anything and not to take things personally.

**We all have the power to control how we allow ourselves to respond or react to any given situation. No one can make you feel any emotion unless you decide to allow yourself to feel that way.

**Becoming aware of your thoughts is the first step to becoming the observer.

**Becoming the observer allows you the time needed to not react.

**Being in the present moment aligns you with the true nature of reality.

**Mindfulness involves being in a present state of awareness.

**Focusing on your breath brings you into the present moment.

**Taking personal responsibility for oneself is the key to self-empowerment.

**Your gut feelings and intuition are never wrong, because they are messages from your higher expanded self.

**Your higher expanded self is always connected to you and is the part of you that is not physical.

2

Eventually, the ocean receded after leaving behind the elements of its massive destruction and relocating much of the native population of Spark's homeland. There was an eerie silence—the calm after the storm.

Several days later, on a distant beach, a saturated bird's nest washed up onto the sand. There, nestled deep in the crevice between

the twisted twigs, was a scared, exhausted, and alive Spark. She awakened and found herself confused, alone, and in unfamiliar surroundings. Spark was overcome with sadness. She had lost everything: family, friends, community, and the safety of her home— all taken from her in a matter of minutes.

Although this experience was devastating, this was not the first time Spark had had to overcome tremendous pain while grappling with how to survive a near-death experience. In the midst of such grief, she suddenly found herself reflecting upon an old memory. She recalled an unusually cold winter with freezing temperatures. It was so cold that many in her community froze to death. Slipping in and out of consciousness and nearly freezing to death, Spark was so close to dying that all she had was the present moment. Having learned through paying attention to her thoughts how to become the observer and, thus, connect with her higher expanded self, she was able, in that moment,

to hear the whisper in her own voice that told her the truth: **"If you always go within, you will never go without. Abundance is within.** *Don't be afraid. You can help heal yourself."* *In that life-or-death moment, Spark was no longer preoccupied with thoughts of the past or fantasies of the future, and she had the ability to hear the faint whisper of her inner voice. That whisper emanating from Spark's own forgotten wisdom, coming from her higher expanded self, told her what to do.*

Spark first concentrated on controlling her breathing and her heartbeat, which she sped up to increase the blood flow and circulation. Next, Spark visualized a ball of light expanding within her. As the ball of light expanded more and more in size, energy was produced, warming her up from the inside. She realized that by using her willful focus, she was able to not only create this ball but also make it as big or small as she wanted and move it throughout her inner body.

At that time, she realized even more that within her was a power beyond her current understanding. That was when she came to know that there were two Sparks: her normal, everyday self and the part of her that existed in a higher place of infinite wisdom, or her higher expanded self. Her normal, everyday self was always connected to her higher expanded self. With time, Spark completely recovered from her near-death experience in the cold. She continued, in her moments of silence, to hear, trust, and be guided by her higher expanded self.

As Spark lay within the crumpled twigs, washed up upon the beach of a foreign land, she found herself remembering the truth: **"If you always go within, you will never go without. Abundance**

is within." She allowed herself to trust and rely on her faith in the knowledge that her trouble wouldn't last. *This too shall pass,* she repeated to herself over and over in her head. This calmed her thoughts and allowed Spark to assess her situation, garner strength, and muster up the courage to venture out into the forest for food and shelter before dark. Finding a tree with luscious green leaves upon it, she ate her first meal in many days.

Emotionally overwhelmed, Spark gave in to the relentless tiredness she felt and tried to quiet her restless mind by comforting herself. As she quieted her thoughts, she heard that same soft whisper reminding her of what her grandmother had told her: "**The truth is that separateness is an illusion, and we are never alone.**" Spark thought, *How could that possibly be? I have never felt as alone as I do right now.* Spark then dozed off and began to dream. In her dream, she saw her family surrounding her, and she felt their love as she fell even deeper into sleep.

As Spark continued to sleep, she dreamed of a magnificent apple orchard. In the orchard, one particular tree caught her eye. Hanging from the branches of the tree were apples that sparkled with a brilliant array of colors. The tree's leaves were vibrant, in beautiful shades of green. The pieces of fruit were so large that it appeared the branches were struggling to hold their weight and keep them from touching the ground. Although there was no wind, she noticed the tree branches start to sway. Suddenly, Spark felt as if she were being watched, and she looked up and saw that the tree was smiling at her.

Spark thought, *How are you able to create such lovely fruit that looks so different from you?*

In that moment, an apple dropped down to the ground, rolled over to Spark, and split in half.

The tree said, "See those seeds? Those seeds created me, and I created the apple. The essence of the tree, the apple, and the seed are all contained within each other, no matter how you slice it."

Spark smiled and giggled at the humor, which reminded her of her father's humor. She said, "So it's true when they say that the apple doesn't fall too far from the tree. But how come you all look so different from each other?"

The tree shook, letting out a little laugh. "Looks can be deceiving. It's only an illusion. The apple looks so different not only from the seed but also from me. But within the apple are seeds that, when planted, become a tree."

In that moment, Spark had a vision of her siblings and asked, "How is it that each of us is so different, and we all have the same parents?"

*The tree said, "You each have your individuality, although you come from the same source. You are connected not only to your siblings, who appear to be physically separate from you, but also to everyone and everything, no matter how different they may look from you. Spark, the truth is, **we are eternal and are all one**."*

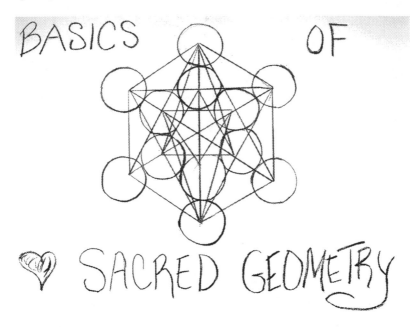

BASICS OF

♡ SACRED GEOMETRY

Spark said, "So it may appear that we are different and separate, yet you are saying we are all one? How is it that you, the tree, and I, a caterpillar, are one, the same, or even connected?"

The tree said, *"I, you, the apple, the seed, and everything else in existence are connected because we all sprang forth from the same source, and that's why we all consist of the same substance. Everything is composed of extremely tiny particles of light vibrating at different frequencies. These particles are so small that they cannot be seen with the naked eye."*

Spark asked, *"Are you saying that if everything and everyone in creation was broken down to its smallest parts, exposing its truest essence, all that would remain is colorful, vibrating light?"*

"Yes, after all the physical form and dense matter is stripped away, all that would be left is the same exact light."

Spark said, *"So you're saying that because we are all composed of the same substance, light, we are all one?"*

"Exactly!"

Suddenly, she remembered that in the past, when she had felt alone and cried out for comfort, in that moment, she'd begun to feel warmth within, as if she were no longer alone. Her thoughts had turned to her deceased aunt and grandfather, and she'd known it was their love. At that time, when she'd shared her experience with her grandmother, her grandmother had explained that at any time, one could call on loved ones who had passed away and left the physical world for guidance and comfort.

Spark was intrigued. "Would you explain some more about this light?"

The tree said, "These divine sparks of light are energy that exist in every living being. They are intelligent, alive, and immortal and have their own awareness. They can never be extinguished. This is not at all possible."

"So this light or energy can never be destroyed?"

The tree said, "Exactly. It can only be transformed. Furthermore, even if the particles are separated by great distances, these particles of light always stay in constant communication with every other particle of light."

"How are they able to do this?"

"Because they are connected by an invisible force that entangles all things."

Spark said, "So everything is connected by this invisible force? What's this force that none of us can even see?"

"The invisible force connecting everything is consciousness, awareness of one's self."

Spark said, "It's hard to understand how something so small and as intangible as light can be aware of itself."

The tree said, *"The particles are self-aware because they are the building blocks of existence. They are not taking part in the illusion of separation and playing the game of hide-and-seek. Because the particles' ability to know their true essence is not purposefully blocked."*

Spark said, *"I don't understand. What do you mean by the illusion of separation and the game of hide-and-seek?"*

The tree said, *"It is only a metaphor. Like in the game we play as young ones, where one player seeks out the hiding places of the other players. In our game of hide-and-seek, each of us is our own seeker, and we seek to find the hidden nature of our true essence."*

"How does that happen?"

"Our reality is orchestrated purposefully to appear separate, random, and chaotic and give the illusion of certain aspects

being hidden. It is designed this way to provide the framework in which one can seek out the true nature of reality. In other words, there is a reason that everyone is unaware of who he or she truly is."

Spark said, "So everyone is living with and operating under a type of amnesia?"

"That's exactly what it is. A sort of forgetfulness has been purposely placed over the consciousness of everyone."

Spark said, "This world is sometimes so painful. Who would design this purposefully? Why do you refer to it as a game of hide-and-seek, especially when, at times, it is not fun at all?"

The tree said, "You, I, and everyone else designed the true nature of life on earth purposefully to be hidden so that we would then seek to uncover the true nature of reality. The allures of the physical senses and the physical world often distract and preoccupy our attention and make us feel separate from each other. The goal of the game is to seek and ultimately remember that at our core, we are infinitely powerful beings of love and light and are engaged in a game with ourselves to see if we can fool ourselves by hiding and forgetting who and what we really are. This process, which is filled with infinite possibilities and unlimited probabilities, allows for rapid growth and expansion. We have designed the physical world to be the game board as we play our game of hide-and-seek."

Spark said, "That we willingly agreed to participate in this game and experience the illusion of separateness is difficult to come to terms with."

"I know, but ultimately, we are the willing participants and designers of this game. The good news is that each divine spark contained in a physical body is at all times in a state of constant connection and communication with its higher expanded self."

Spark said, "Does our higher expanded self experience the illusion of separateness?"

"Actually, no. Our higher expanded self exists outside the game of hide-and-seek. It watches our progress and offers help and guidance when appropriate. The help and guidance are offered subtly through our intuition and gut feelings, as well as by other means of communication."

Spark said, "Oh, wow, that's so true! I remember my grandmother always told me to learn to listen to the soft voice within, which says, **'If you always go within, you will never go without. Abundance is within**.' But what I don't understand is this: How does the physical *part of me that is engaged in playing the game of hide-and-seek work with my higher expanded self in creating the reality I live in?"*

"Maybe the best way to explain the relationship between the physical part and the higher expanded self is in a visualization. Imagine a vast, endless, untapped field of potential energy. This field of energy contains an infinite and abundant source of powerful, creative force. The potential energy in this field lies dormant until one's consciousness is directed upon it."

Spark asked, "How is a person's consciousness directed upon the field?"

The tree said, "Our consciousness is directed upon the field by our emotions. Our emotions are energy in motion and directly fuel what we experience in our reality."

Spark said, *"So what I think and feel, whether it is positive or negative, draws that into my reality?"*

"Yes. If we align our beliefs and emotions with a desired or undesired outcome, it speeds up the physical formation of that outcome into our reality."

"So does that mean I have total control of the outcome through what I believe and feel?" Spark asked.

"Well, Spark, it's not that simple. There is more than just your limited self involved in the outcome. The dreams, desires, and wants of a conscious being who is living in illusion and engaged in playing the game of hide-and-seek is at all times in connection with his or her higher expanded self. And that higher expanded self delivers to the limited self playing the game the measure of fulfillment consistent with and in line with the feelings and vibration of that limited self's current, at-the-moment level of consciousness.

"By expanding one's level of consciousness and residing in that expanded state, one interacts with the field of potential energy, and the physical creations that then spring forth from the field are an exact vibratory match to the level of consciousness currently residing within the individual playing the game of hide and seek."

Spark said, *"Oh my gosh, I just lost everything and everyone, so how am I to believe and trust that things will work out for my best interest?"*

The tree said, *"Well, I know it is difficult to imagine why this would all be purposefully orchestrated, and it is even harder to comprehend the whole picture when you are in pain and viewing life from your pain and the illusion of separation. However, things will only happen at the time they are most appropriate to further one's spiritual development. From a limited perspective, life only appears to be separate, random, and chaotic, and that perspective is the source of your pain. It is important, Spark, to go within and listen to that soft voice."*

Spark said, "Sounds like learning to trust our higher expanded self to know the bigger picture is essential in order to go through our healing process and to grow. I guess in time, I will begin to understand what all of this is supposed to teach me. But would you please remind me again—who purposefully orchestrated this reality?"

"Each of us is responsible for the design of and participation in our experiences in creating our reality, in cooperation with our higher expanded selves."

"Are you saying I am responsible for everything in my life, including the storm?"

The tree said, "Well, Spark, I know it is hard to fathom, but absolutely. Your true essence created the storm as a catalyst to create the opportunity to experience extreme adversity. From your same expanded awareness, there is a knowing that nothing is bad or good. Oftentimes, the greatest growth and expansion in consciousness occur as a result of tremendous hardship and chaos."

"Our higher expanded self sees the pain and hardship differently?" Spark said.

"Yes, because our true essence consists of an infinite, all-powerful, abundant energy that can never be extinguished. It is not part of, or affected by, the physical aspects of the physical world. To our higher expanded selves, hardship is an illusion and simply a teaching tool for the physical aspect of ourselves."

Spark looked confused. "When you say 'true essence,' what is it you are referring to?"

The tree said, "One's spirit, divine spark, higher expanded self, soul, and many more are all names used to define our true essence. As all-powerful, immortal, and abundant beings, we have agreed out of love to engage in a game of hide-and-seek by purposefully forgetting and intentionally placing a veil over our memory so that we may assist in the expansion of all there is."

"Are you saying that the only reason we are here playing hide-and-seek is to assist in the expansion of all there is?"

The tree said, "It's not the only reason, but it's one of them. We also created such a wonderful landscape so we could experience the joy of having new experiences."

Spark was a bit more confused. "I am still not totally clear about what the goal or purpose is of agreeing to go through all this without remembering we agreed to it in the first place."

"The ultimate goal is to become conscious co-creators of our lives and create and experience our greatest dreams on earth, while still keeping a keen awareness of the true nature of reality."

Spark shook her head, still confused. *"Why would we want to forget? I'm still not clear as to why we would agree to play this game."*

"Because it creates an unknown that can be made known. When you experience something for the first time, how that is experienced is new. You are experiencing something you have never experienced before. You would experience this physical world completely differently as an all-knowing, abundant, immortal being instead of a veiled, limited, mortal being."

Spark said, *"We agreed to all of this just to experience it?"*

"Yes, so we can experience the joy of remembering through the process of playing the game of life on earth. Like I mentioned

before, we are at all times connected to our higher expanded self. The illusion is made possible because of the veil of forgetfulness that we agreed to have placed over our memory. As we live our lives on earth, most of us never remember that we are infinite, abundant, and immortal beings. We get lost in the illusions of the physical world and in the dramas of our lives."

Spark was beginning to grasp the idea of agreeing to play the game of hide-and-seek. "What happens once we begin to remember and awaken to our true essence?"

The tree said, "It is quite profound and very powerful when we remember our true essence and the fact that we are immortal, powerful, and abundant, because we are then able to reclaim our power and tap into the real abundance of our natural selves."

"Wow, that sounds incredible! How are we able to reclaim our power?"

The tree said, "As we begin to change our perception by remembering our true state of abundance and as we remember our true state, our entire reality changes accordingly."

"So are you saying that our perception of ourselves impacts our reality?"

"Yes, greatly! The outer life is always a reflection of the inner, so the more abundance we feel as we connect with our higher expanded self, the more abundance is reflected in our lives."

"So wouldn't our beliefs be important?" Spark asked.

"Very much so. Our limited beliefs create a filter. Those who are willing to withdraw all the power from their limited beliefs and change their perception of reality are able to tap into the true power of their natural and immortal self."

Spark said, "Let me see if I understand. Are you saying that instead of being influenced by our higher expanded self, we have forgotten who we truly are and instead are influenced by our beliefs, which are completely influenced by the illusion?"

"Yes, we are totally influenced by our beliefs. We have a filter that provides understanding to our reality. This filter is woven together from our family's influence, our environment, and all of our experiences, which, over time, create an automatic belief system—a belief system in which everything we experience is affected by this filter."

"What do you mean that everything is affected by this filter? Are our thoughts, emotions, words, and actions affected by the filter?"

"Absolutely. Our belief system provides us with a perception of reality that directly influences our thoughts, emotions, and actions. If our perception, beliefs, and filter are limited, we are left with a *perception of reality that is fundamentally based upon the concept of duality and polar opposites, one of conflict and division."*

Spark was still not convinced. "It is still pretty hard for me to grasp why we would knowingly agree to experience conflict and division."

*The tree said, "Sometimes it is hard for me too. However, we agreed to participate in this grand illusion of duality because the truth is, **duality provides the opportunity to grow, and expressing gratitude enhances that growth."***

Spark said, "I don't understand. What do you mean by duality?"

The tree said, "Duality means 'having two parts.' To understand duality, it helps to understand its opposite—unity. In unity, everything exists as a complete oneness."

"Is duality a part of unity?"

"Yes, everything in existence is a part of unity, including the illusion of duality. Duality is simply a created fiction that allows us to expand and grow on a personal level while we play the game of hide-and-seek."

Spark asked, "Can you give me an example?"

The tree said, "For example, when one experiences what love isn't in order to truly know what love is."

Spark was trying to digest the information. "Am I to understand that it's the duality that gives the illusion of separateness, which is provided by the environment within which we all operate, because it is designed for us to experience opposites?"

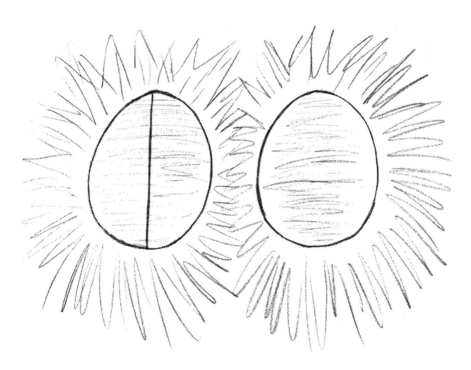

The tree said, "Yes, the duality is only an illusion. In truth, there is no separation, no difference, and no disconnectedness in unity. In unity, because all is one, everything is known at once, and what is

known by one is also immediately known by all in this connected state. Alternatively, what is known by one is not known by all in duality."

Spark asked, "When or how do we experience this state of unity?"

"By permanently shifting our perspective away from duality consciousness toward unity consciousness. Only in duality are we able to have this type of learning experience. Only by experiencing one's opposite do we truly recognize and appreciate the other. There would be no appreciation of beauty without the existence of ugliness, no appreciation of good without the understanding of bad, no appreciation of love without the existence of fear, and no comprehension of unity without the experiences of living and struggling in duality."

Spark said, "It sounds like you're saying that all I have been through is for my growth."

"Yes. Challenges are the catalyst and provide the opportunities to allow us to discover more of who we are. Spark, living with challenges allows us to reach for our highest potential. That is when we are given an opportunity to become active participants in a game of our own making. A life without challenge would soon become boring and monotonous. Imagine playing a game of cards and knowing everyone else's hand. At first, it might be enjoyable, but at some point, the game would grow boring because there would be no ability to be surprised and no ability to be challenged."

Spark asked, "Why would we choose for bad things to happen to us? Why wouldn't we just choose good things?"

The tree said, "It is by design that we are exposed to a multitude of circumstances in order to add to existence. Judging whether an obstacle is good or bad limits our perception of the experience. By judging anything, we are focusing our thoughts and emotions, which have tremendous power and influence. Our perception determines the way in which we ultimately overcome that challenge. Once the judgment is fixed, we are then in a more difficult position to release the judgment and overcome the obstacle."

Spark said, "If we have judgment about something, how do we release our judgment?"

"We do the opposite. Since judgments stem from the belief that we are separate from each other and from the source of all things, the way to release that limiting belief is to embrace the truth that we are all one."

"Okay, how do we do that? You make it sound so simple."

"It is, but for many, it is not easy. It is done through the expression of gratitude. One of the laws of our universe is that like attracts like. Similar to a snowball effect, when one is in a state of gratitude, that energy and vibration is sent out and gathers to it all equivalent

energies of appreciation. The accumulated energy of gratitude then revisits the sender and delivers a more abundant state of gratitude. The emotion of gratitude is a vibration of energy that diminishes judgment and attracts new possibilities. When one is always living in a state of gratitude, one is constantly receiving the inflow and outflow of benevolent energy. In this state, it is possible to see challenges not with a judgmental eye but with the deep knowing that each challenge is appropriate and simply a teaching tool to be appreciated."

Spark asked, "Does the law that like attracts like only apply to those who know of it?"

"No, universal laws operate regardless of whether one is aware of them or not. That's because everyone and everything is created from the same essential substance."

"What is that substance?"

The tree smiled. "Loving light."

In that moment, Spark realized that her notions that the physical world was all there was and that a person was born alone and died alone were simply limiting beliefs. The realization that beings were not separate and that she was never alone gave her a tremendous amount of comfort. The message resonated so deeply within her that she knew it was the truth. She had always known it, but in her time of pain, she had momentarily forgotten. With that remembrance, the dream ended, and Spark fell into a deeper sleep.

When morning broke, Spark reflected upon her dream. It occurred to Spark that she had always had a special relationship with trees. She recalled a time in her childhood when another storm had taken down many of the oldest and most unyielding and rigid trees, leaving standing and unhurt those trees that appeared to be more vulnerable with their supple branches. She realized that the trees that were torn down from the storm refused to bend in the face of the mighty winds, and those trees that survived were flexible in their ability to bend with the ever-changing circumstances. It was the surviving trees' ability to go with the flow that allowed those trees to survive and thrive during and after the storm. From that experience, Spark learned that her willingness to be flexible and bend would provide her with the greatest strength in dealing with each and every moment.

Chapter 2 Highlights

**The truth is, if you always go within, you will never go without. Abundance is within.

**Our normal everyday self is always connected to our higher expanded self.

**The truth is, separateness is an illusion, and we are never alone.

**The truth is, we are eternal and are all one.

**Everything in creation is connected, because we all sprang forth from the same source. That's why we all consist of the same substance.

**Everything is composed of extremely tiny particles of light.

**Consciousness is the invisible force that connects all things.

**Life is really a game of hide-and-seek. The truths are hidden, and our job is to seek them out.

**The higher expanded self exists outside the game of hide-and-seek.

**Our emotions are energy in motion and directly fuel manifestation.

**Thoughts and feelings, whether positive or negative, influence our reality.

3

As Spark started her day in this new place, although she was still exhausted from all the trauma she had been through, she took a moment to witness the sun radiating its nourishing light upon the awakening wildlife and flora of the forest. In that moment, shifting her perspective allowed her to be present and notice the sunlight reflecting off the morning dew, causing all that it touched to glisten, creating a painting of a beautiful spectrum of light. The sounds made by the critters as they awoke resembled a grand orchestra performing an elaborate symphony. Spark remembered her dream and gathered up enough gratitude to think about how beautiful the forest looked. Spark then heard the sound of crackling leaves, and she noticed a sight she had never seen before. On a limb directly above her head, a beautiful iridescent butterfly emerged from its cocoon.

Up on a tree branch of an ancient sequoia, a butterfly named Omni emerged from its slumber to create its day and greet the morning. Omni was aware and already had a deep knowing of the true nature of reality. Omni knew that when one was coming from love versus fear, that emotion was the underlying influence and intention that colored the end result.

Knowing one's intentions was key. Simply asking oneself, "Am I making this choice from love or fear?" allowed one to become aware of his or her true intentions. When one was operating from a place of love, balance was created. The truth was, according to Omni, **"Thinking with our hearts and feeling with our heads allows for balance."** Omni was aware that one's intentions were the blueprint and driving force of how one experienced one's reality. Ultimately, *one's motivation and intention were what fueled the nature and outcome of an experience.*

Omni fluttered above Spark as Spark looked up.

Omni said, "How we interpret and respond to an experience not only influences the experience but also determines how the outcome unfolds for the individual from the experience. Learn to be mindful of love and lead with love. For example, when your sister was upset and took her frustrations out on you, if you had not taken it personally and had seen that she was obviously upset, you could have comforted her instead of getting angry. That would have changed the way you experienced that interaction."

Notwithstanding the wisdom Spark had gained through her experiences, she suddenly felt the loss of all her loved ones wash over her, and she wished her family could be there to share the beauty. She began to uncontrollably sob. Omni, seeing her cry, fluttered down and landed next to Spark.

Omni, in a compassionate voice, said, "Spark, I am so sorry for your pain."

Spark calmed down and, puzzled, looked at Omni. "Do I know you?" Without waiting for an answer, looking up at the cocoon, she asked, "What is that? Is that where you live?"

Omni said, "You mean the cocoon? Yes. I lived there only temporarily, though, because it is such an important part of life's process."

Spark asked, "Why is it such an important part of life's process?"

Omni said, "The cocoon allows us to go deep within to transform all that no longer serves us. By quieting the outer world, it enables us to experience the true nature of reality as we allow ourselves to be guided by our inner wisdom."

Spark said, "So does everyone go through this process?"

"Everybody will eventually."

"Why is it so important to know about the true nature of reality?"

Omni said, "Understanding the true nature of reality allows us to take our blinders off and see through the illusion."

"What illusion?" Spark asked.

"*Time, for instance, is a grand illusion. Once one is able to understand that linear time—in which there is a past, present, and future—is a purposefully designed tool, one is able to know the truth that everything in creation is ultimately happening now, all in the present moment. All time streams are happening at once, so the only thing that exists is the present moment. The illusion of linear time exists because it serves an important function.*"

Spark shook her head. "Now I am more confused. How is everything happening now, when I know I experienced many things before this moment?"

Omni said, "I know it's confusing, Spark, but that's because the linear mind is just that—linear and limited, and it sees things as such. However, as you have learned from your grandmother and the tree, you are not just your mind or limited self; you are also your higher expanded self. Everything is happening now because nothing exists until, by observation, our consciousness is directed upon it."

Spark asked, "How does that work when it comes to time?"

Omni said, "Ultimately, linear time is a function of consciousness, a way to allow objective reality to unfold."

"Oh. Although it appears that something already happened, it is only happening now if I think about it now?"

*"Yes, everything is happening now because things only come into being when they are observed by our consciousness. Always remember that our consciousness is totally influenced by our perspective. Where our perspective is formed and how we observe our reality is directly influenced by our own expectations and beliefs. Because, Spark, as you remember, the truth is, **you create your reality; your outer world is a reflection of your inner world.***

"Understanding that we create our reality allows us to experience our own personal power and in turn provides the ability to consciously make choices when navigating our life."

Spark said, *"So what happens once I begin to transform myself by making conscious choices?"*

Omni said, *"One of the gifts of transformation is the ability to become more open. It allows us access to greater insight and universal wisdom, ultimately bringing peace of mind in life's most tragic and fearful moments."*

"How does it do that?"

"When we understand and accept that what is happening is appropriate and learn to trust that everything that happens is for our highest and best good, then we are able to navigate the ebb and flow of life more effectively while simultaneously being a conscious creator of our reality. Also, because our perception is what determines our interpretation of our experiences, when we, in this now moment, perceive our past from our expanded higher selves' consciousness, we are given a different understanding, and that changes our perception of our experience of the past."

Spark said, *"How do you know this to be true?"*

"Because I have learned through the process of remembering and have removed the veil of forgetfulness, thereby allowing myself to have a broader perspective of how true reality operates.

"From your perspective, living under leaves and branches, your ability to see the totality of your reality is blocked. But from a different perspective, one in which nothing is blocked, one is able to know and see much more of the bigger picture." Omni turned to Spark. "Would you like me to show you?"

In a state of awe, before Spark even finished uttering the word yes, she found herself being lifted up onto the wings of Omni. Spark, for the first time, felt free from the limitations of her present state. As they continued to fly higher and higher, Spark noticed that she was able to observe more and more of her environment, and she started to understand how limited in scope her previous perception was. She thought, This is all so serene and beautiful.

Suddenly, Omni started a downward spiral. Before Spark was aware of what was happening, she felt Omni land and was surrounded by darkness. Unfortunately, being in complete darkness brought into Spark's mind the familiar emotion of fear once again and brought her back to the horrifying experience of battling the storm. Before she had time to speak, Omni said, "It's okay—there's no need to be afraid. Just breathe, be patient, and watch."

Spark, hearing Omni's words, took a deep breath and began to feel calm. Within seconds, two pinpoints of light appeared, revealing themselves as fireflies. Instantly, they illuminated a shiny and jagged surface.

Omni asked, "Can you see what is in front of us?"

Spark said, "Yes, a jagged and shiny surface."

"Can you see anything else?"

Spark tried to please Omni by seeing something but saw nothing else. "No, it's too dark."

Omni then uttered a sound, and like magic, the darkness completely disappeared. The entire space was illuminated by thousands of flickering fireflies. Spark realized she was inside a cave constructed of magnificent crystals.

Omni said, "Spark, do you realize that a moment ago, it appeared that we were alone? Yet when light illuminated the darkness, the true reality appeared: thousands of fireflies and these magnificent crystals surround us. Our five senses are not able to perceive the whole picture. Therefore, as we increase our inner light, our ability to perceive the true nature of all things expands."

Spark said, "So you are saying that everything is not always as it seems?"

Omni said, "Yes, everything in creation is in a constant state of movement and varying degrees of vibration and harmonic frequency. Our physical senses are not capable of recognizing all of these vibrations and frequencies. That is why things are not always as they seem, Spark, and that is also why your perception is what matters most. When you think you are only your limited self and operate from that perspective, your life is experienced according to *your beliefs and expectations. However, when you learn to become the observer and allow your higher expanded self to be your guide, it is life changing.*

"You also know from your past that within you are a light and energy that you can control. When you shift your perception and let go of fear, by surrendering to the present moment and trusting your intuition, you recognize your authentic true power."

Spark said, "That is so true! By my trusting and accepting what was happening, everything changed."

"Exactly. It was your trust and acceptance that allowed you to connect with your inner light and taught you that you are never alone. What you are still learning to do is to release limiting beliefs that no longer serve you."

Spark said, "Thank you for reminding me."

After Spark's expression of gratitude, Omni lifted her up onto her wings, and in what seemed like no time at all, Spark found herself back on the branch where they'd first met. After Spark was safely delivered back to her new environment, Omni flew away, reassuring Spark, "I am just a thought away."

*Spark felt comforted as she reflected upon the day's events, and she finally understood the truth, which she spoke aloud: "**Love is the blueprint of creation; fear blocks our authentic power.**"*

In this time of reflection, Spark found strength and peace in knowing that her authentic power came directly from her ability to connect with her higher expanded self.

Chapter 3 Highlights

**Love and fear are the underlying influences and intentions that color each and every experience in our life.

The truth is, thinking with our hearts and feeling with our heads allows for balance.

**One's intentions are the blueprint and driving force of how one experiences reality.

**Quieting the outer world enables us to experience our inner world, the true nature of reality.

**Everything in creation is ultimately happening now, in the present moment.

**Time is a function of consciousness, a way to allow the unfolding of manifestation and objective reality.

**Our expectations and beliefs shape our perspective, which directly influences how we observe our reality.

The truth is, you create your reality; your outer world is a reflection of your inner world.

**Everything that happens to us is appropriate and is happening for our highest and best good.

**Our five senses do not perceive the whole picture; therefore, as we increase our inner light, our ability to perceive the true nature of all things expands.

**Everything in creation is in a constant state of movement and varying degrees of vibration and frequencies. Our five physical senses cannot recognize all of these vibrations and frequencies.

**Surrendering to the present moment and trusting your intuition connect you to your authentic, true power.

**The truth is, love is the blueprint of creation; fear blocks our authentic power.

4

Spark, with new insight, stretched her legs and went out in search of her morning snack. She was so deep in her thoughts about what had happened over the past few days that she almost stumbled over a pair of quarreling caterpillars named Dusky and Dawny, who were so preoccupied that they didn't notice her. It soon became apparent to Spark what they were arguing about.

Dusky was crying while pointing at a cocoon hanging from a branch and blaming Dawny for something. "It's your fault! If you hadn't—"

Interrupting them, Spark raised her voice enough to be heard. "Hey, is there anything I can do to help?"

Alarmed, they stopped fighting, turned toward Spark, and stared in disbelief.

Spark said, "Is everything all right?"

Dusky said, "Isn't it obvious that it's not? What do you think? Look what has happened to our sister." Dusky and Dawny's sister was suspended from a nearby tree and wrapped up in a cocoon.

"I told Dawny we never should have taken this trail."

Spark said, "What do you mean you never should have taken this trail? Why does that matter?"

Dawny said, "Well, as soon as we got on this path, this bizarre thing started to happen to our kid sister. Dusky is blaming me, saying that she ate some kind of poison and now is dying."

Spark, knowing that this was a part of the process of life, broke into a little smile. "Oh no, we all eventually go through this natural process of life. Change is inevitable. We are forever changing. Learning to embrace change makes living in this world much easier. Your sister is not dying. She is transforming into something even grander."

Dawny said, "So you are saying this is normal?"

"Yes, it is normal. Prior to this, did you notice anything different about her?"

Dusky said, "She seemed to be going through some kind of change. She was tired, and she stopped participating in our usual gossip and banter. All she wanted to do was spend quiet time alone, and she asked weird questions that didn't interest us. She kept saying, 'Who am I? What am I? What's my purpose?'"

Dawny interrupted. "It wasn't that I wasn't interested. It's just that as her older brother, I found myself in the unfamiliar position of not having the answers."

Dusky jumped back in, annoyed. "Okay, well, then I wasn't interested either. Who really cares anyway?"

Spark kindly looked at both of them to attempt to ease their concerns and fear. "What I think may be happening is that these questions being asked by your sister started a process of change and transformation within her. I have learned that oftentimes, the distractions of the outer world inhibit our ability to quiet ourselves enough to allow us to listen to our inner guidance. The cocoon provides the opportunity for solitude and represents our willingness and courage to go within and explore the unknown."

Dawny was becoming slightly enamored with Spark and smiled. Spark had an attraction to Dawny as well.

Dawny said, "That makes sense."

Spark smiled back at Dawny.

Dusky said, "What the heck are you both talking about?"

Dawny, admiring Spark, asked, "Is there anything else you can share that would help us to better wrap our legs around these ideas?"

Spark batted her eyelashes at Dawny and crossed half her legs. She was beginning to feel things she had never felt before.

Spark said, "Maybe this story will help. When I was a young caterpillar, I nearly froze to death."

Upon hearing the word death, both Dawny and Dusky turned their full attention to Spark.

*Spark continued. "That experience was intense. Yet it gave me the opportunity to know that the truth is, **if you always go within, you will never go without. Abundance is within.**"*

Dusky was even more confused. "Huh? Go where?"

Spark said, "How about this? Close your eyes, and think about a lush green forest with all the delicious leaves you could possibly eat."

Dusky closed his eyes and began to smile.

Spark said, "Okay, so why did you do that?"

Dusky said, "Do what?"

"Why did you smile? What emotion were you feeling?"

Dusky said, "I smiled because I was imagining what you said."

Spark said, "How did you feel when you thought about the lush forest and smiled?"

Dusky said, "It felt good."

"Okay, where were you imagining it?"

Dusky said, "Inside my head, of course. That's a silly question."

*Spark said, "So that is how you begin to go within. You begin by learning to be mindful and aware of your thoughts. Your thoughts are significant, because the truth is, **you create your reality; your outer world is a reflection of your inner world."***

Dusky said, "You're kidding me! You are saying our thoughts are what create our reality?"

Spark said, "Yes, exactly; however, our thoughts are not the only thing that creates our reality. Our reality is actually created by two different complementary actions. One consists of our thoughts and emotions from our limited self, which projects energy that influences our experiences. The other is our higher expanded self, which is in a constant state of loving its limited self and delivering its full measure of truth and love to the limited self. The limited self, however, can receive only the amount of truth and love that it has allowed itself to hold. It is the current level of consciousness exhibited by the limited self that determines how much fulfillment may be received from the higher expanded self. The more expanded the limited self allows itself to be in terms of raising its consciousness, the more fulfillment it receives."

Dawny said, "How exactly would one go about creating his or her reality, and how does one manage to do that when we have so many different thoughts?"

Spark said, "What I do first is start to pay attention to how I feel. Our feelings are extremely important because they come from the thoughts we are consciously or unconsciously choosing to focus upon. Our thoughts are so powerful that we have the power to create a dream state for ourselves or a nightmare. I have come to understand that our thoughts and emotions can produce imbalances and disease or health and well-being, depending upon where we choose to place our attention."

Dawny said, "This is a lot to grasp. Maybe you can give us an example."

Spark said, *"Sure. Do this: think about a time when you felt most happy."*

Dawny said, *"Okay."*

Spark said, *"Now tell us about what you are thinking about."*

"I am thinking about when I was younger, and our whole family would go to the pond and play for hours. We would play till we were exhausted, but we were so happy."

Spark said, *"Okay, so how do you feel when thinking about it now?"*

Dawny said, *"Joyful. Oh, now I get it: when I focus my thoughts, I then begin to feel."*

Spark said, *"Exactly. Reflecting on that day, does your heart feel heavy or lighter?"*

Dawny thought for a moment. *"Lighter, I guess."*

Spark looked over to Dusky and noticed tears running down his face, she turned her attention to him. "What are you thinking?"

Dusky said, "Thinking about those times makes me really sad. It makes my heart feel heavy because I miss our parents."

Dawny said, "Hey, I miss our parents too, but I was choosing to focus on something that makes me feel good, and you chose to focus on Mom and Dad being gone."

Spark said, "Do you see how your feelings are determined by your thoughts?"

Dawny and Dusky nodded. Spark couldn't seem to stop looking at Dawny, and she noticed that her fond feelings toward him were growing. Dawny was feeling the same way, and it was becoming obvious to both of them, but neither said anything. She smiled and looked at Dusky, trying not to make her feelings obvious to Dusky.

Spark said, "Dawny chose to focus on happy thoughts to feel uplifted, and you chose to think about heavy ones. Using myself as an example, when I think of the circumstances in my life at this moment, I do not feel profound sadness, because I understand that from an expanded higher perspective, I agreed out of love to go through what I have gone through."

Dawny said, "How did you get your expanded perspective?"

*Spark said, "My expanded perspective has come from my personal internal work and life experiences, which have brought me to know the truth that **duality provides the opportunity to grow, and expressing gratitude enhances that growth.**"*

Dusky said, "Okay, so we get to choose what thoughts we want to put our attention on, and then how we feel comes from that choice?"

Spark said, "Exactly!"

Dawny said, "I can understand the power of our thoughts and feelings, but why would we agree out of love to go through so much pain?"

"Because from a more expanded perspective, one in which we are fully experiencing the connection to the love of everything in existence, we know and trust that any pain is temporary. It is based on the illusion of the duality of the physical world and is ultimately appropriate for the expansion of everything in existence."

Dawny said, "Wow, I'd love to fully experience the connection to the love of creation. How does one go about shifting to a more expanded perspective?"

Spark looked at Dawny with excitement and gratitude. She felt blessed that she had met someone she was attracted to who was interested in what she was interested in.

Spark said, "Making a decision to become aware of what we are thinking and then learning to observe our thoughts are how we begin to separate ourselves from the repetitive thoughts that our limited self generates. Being the observer allows us to notice we are not just our thoughts. Through the silence, we begin to hear the whisper of our higher expanded self."

Dawny asked, "What can I do to step back from the limiting thoughts I hear in my head?"

Spark said, "Asking ourselves certain questions is a good start. One of the ways I am able to move through an experience in a productive way is by asking myself, 'What is it I am to learn from this experience?' When I quiet my fears by understanding the truth that it is only coming from my limited self and that fear stands for 'false evidence appearing real,' I can then begin to sense or feel the messages from my higher expanded self. As I do this, I open myself up to receive more guidance, which ultimately leads to the creation of a more balanced and peaceful life."

Dawny said, "What you're saying sounds believable. I even got chills when you said the last thing about fear. I do not in any way want to disrespect your knowledge, but how do you really know it's true?"

Spark smiled and shook her head. "No disrespect taken. I am happy to share with you whatever I know. You want to know why I know it's true. It is because I have learned to trust and know that information is truth when receiving it—for instance, when I get a unique physical sensation upon receiving it. Just like the chills you got. Sometimes it occurs as a strong feeling or energy, such as a tug in the pit of my belly. At other times, I too have gotten chills or goose bumps or shivers all over my body. There are even times when I just have a knowing that grows stronger each and every time I continue to listen and trust my inner voice. In addition to all of these, I have also experienced tangible confirmation from my higher expanded self."

Dusky said, "Are you kidding me! Now you are trying to tell us you receive confirmation from yourself? I don't believe you!"

Chapter 4 Highlights

**Distractions of the outer world inhibit our ability to quiet ourselves enough to listen to our inner guidance.

The truth is, if you always go within, you will never go without, since abundance is within.

**Being mindful and aware of your thoughts allows you to go within.

The truth is, you create your reality; your outer world is a reflection of your inner world.

**One's thoughts and emotions can produce imbalances and disease or health and well-being, depending upon where one chooses to focus his or her attention.

The truth is, duality provides the opportunity to grow, and expressing gratitude enhances that growth.

**Pain is a temporary illusion of the duality of the physical world, and it's an appropriate catalyst for the expansion of everything in existence.

**_Fear_ stands for "false evidence appearing real."

5

Upon Dusky's utterance of disbelief, Omni fluttered down from a nearby branch. Spark sensed the presence of Omni and turned to look at her. Dusky and Dawny did as well.

Dusky said, "What the heck is that?"

Dawny said, "Wow, how beautiful. What is it?"

Spark giggled with delight.

Omni floated down to the ground next to all of them.

Omni said, "I represent, as do you, the source of all things. There's no difference between you and me. The truth is, **we are eternal and are all one.** Not only do we come from the same source and just appear different on the outside, but we are, in reality, one singular being expressing itself in a multitude of mental projections. What allows me access to the workings of existence is that I have an awareness of my true essence and origin."

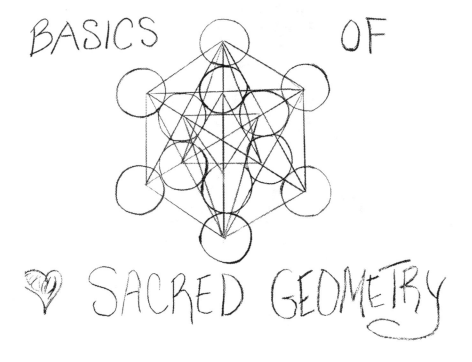

Spark said, "Can you share what your true essence and origin are?"

Omni said, "I am an eternal, infinite, creative, and loving energy force—as are you. This force exists within each and every living and nonliving thing."

Dusky rolled his eyes in frustration at being confused and overwhelmed with the information. He said sarcastically, "You're kidding. That sounds far-fetched. All I have to do is become aware of my true essence and origin—like that is such a simple task—and then once I do that, I have access to the powers that you have? I will be able to know everything and even fly?"

Dawny looked at Dusky and shook his head and then turned to Omni. Dawny was sincerely interested. "How can I become more aware?"

Omni said, "I can understand why this is hard for Dusky to comprehend, because it is not in line with his beliefs. However, to answer your question, Dawny, this process first starts with the desire to become aware. Then one must be willing to take the time to pay attention and learn to observe one's thoughts without judgment. What I mean by not judging your thoughts is noticing them and not labeling them as bad or good or right or wrong."

Dusky was getting more upset at what he was hearing. "Now, what's wrong with judgment? I feel good when I judge other people. It actually gives me pleasure."

Omni said, "That makes sense, as we are all energetic beings, and if we don't feel whole and complete, our energy is lowered. Therefore, when we are judging another, it gives us a temporary energy surge by taking another's energy. Let me ask you this: How do you feel when you are judged or criticized?"

Dusky said, "Well, when you put it that way, come to think of it, not so good when I'm judged. I guess I'm just so used to it that I never paid attention."

Dawny was interested in fully grasping what Spark and Omni were saying. "How does one stop judging oneself?"

Omni said, *"It is a process. By learning to listen to your thoughts and by observing them and developing a level of self-control, you also develop the awareness and the ability to then choose what to focus your attention upon. In that awareness is space to allow one to have the freedom to decide not to judge."*

Dawny said, *"How again do I become aware and learn to observe my thoughts?"*

Omni said, *"By paying attention, you automatically become an observer. It's as if a part of you becomes a fly on the wall, noticing what's occurring."*

Dusky said, *"That seems like a lot of work. What's the benefit?"*

Omni said, *"It's worth it. Switching to the observer perspective allows one to distance themselves from a heightened emotional response. This provides the space and time to not react and to possibly choose differently."*

Dawny said, *"So in a sense, becoming the observer redirects your focus from whatever energy is drawing you in and allows you to see more clearly?"*

Spark, excited that Dawny was comprehending the information, exclaimed, *"Now you're getting it! And by choosing the observer perspective, you can choose to stop judging yourself and others."*

Dusky said, *"Why is it so important to become an observer of your emotions anyway?"*

Omni said, *"Paying attention to your emotions is essential because they are the physical indicator of the specific vibration and frequency associated with your thoughts. Your emotions are energy in motion. Each thought, when broken down to its smallest essence, contains within it photons of light that vibrate in varying degrees of intensity and frequency."*

Dawny said, "Our emotions seem to have so much more influence on our lives than I thought."

*Omni said, "Yes, they do, because the emotion one attaches to a thought is what provides the power to that thought. If you are conscious when a thought pops in, you observe it. If it does not benefit you, you can choose to redirect your thoughts. Learning to come from a loving place instead of reacting from fear changes your reality. Ultimately, the truth is, **thinking with our hearts and feeling with our heads will allow for balance.***

"This is when we begin to expand in consciousness."

Dusky said, "I thought we are all conscious?"

Omni said, "That's true. However, there are different levels of consciousness."

Dusky said, "You mean some people are smarter than others?"

Omni said, "No. How smart one is does not determine how conscious he or she is. The consciousness I am referring to has to do with a level of awareness. Some people are more aware than others. What allows everything to exist is consciousness, and it is woven within the fabric of this reality. It is an important component."

Dawny said, "So that's why my thoughts and feelings are the most important component of mastering my reality?"

Omni said, "Exactly. Every feeling you have is triggered by a conscious or unconscious thought. All you need to remember is to pay close attention to your feelings."

Dawny said, "Once I am feeling something, what do I do then?"

"You may want to ask yourself first what you are feeling. As you realize that you are feeling a certain way—happy, sad, or angry, for instance—you then can reflect by asking yourself what the last thought that triggered that feeling was. For example, the thought of *He betrayed me* leads to the feelings of anger and resentment. The thought of *I am fat* leads to the feelings of shame, guilt, and embarrassment."

Dawny said, "What you're saying is that thoughts come first and then emotions? Then if people can change their thoughts, they can alter their emotions?"

"Exactly." Omni smiled with delight and fluttered her wings excitedly, creating the sound of applause as she fluttered off. As quickly as she'd appeared, she was gone.

Spark said, "Wow, I know it is a lot to absorb."

Dawny said, "I know, but it is good stuff. Spark, we are so blessed that you have come into our lives. I know I will forever be changed."

Spark said, "You are so sweet. I feel very blessed to have met you also. This is such an important process, and it is crucial for you to be patient while going through it and kind to yourself. It allows for the information to be absorbed and become fully integrated."

Chapter 5 Highlights

**The truth is, we are eternal and are all one.

**We come from the same source. We just appear different on the outside.

**Paying attention and learning to observe one's thoughts without judgment bring awareness.

**Becoming the observer allows us to distance ourselves from a heightened emotional response.

**Everything is in a state of vibration and movement. Our emotions are energy in motion.

**The truth is, thinking with our hearts and feeling with our heads will allow for balance.

**Thoughts come first and then emotions. If individuals can change their thoughts, they can alter their emotions.

6

Spark stopped speaking, as she sensed a heavy energy, and then, suddenly, everyone's attention was drawn to a noise in a nearby bush. A shadow emerged from the bush and revealed the presence of an angry, older-looking caterpillar named Gruff.

Gruff shouted, "I can't take any more of your absurdity! I have been listening to your nonsense all day! I have been trying to get away from everything and want to be alone, and then I have to listen to this crap! You have a lot of nerve spreading your new-age mumbo jumbo all over my neck of the woods!"

Spark, immediately recognizing that anger and frustration were just masks to hide one's fear, understood that the antidote to any situation was to respond with love.

Spark said, "We are sorry for disturbing you, sir. We had no idea you were there. Pardon our intrusion."

Gruff said, "Well, at least you apologized for being a disturbance." He calmed down a bit. "Now, leave me alone."

Spark said, "Sir, please. I can sense you are very upset, but why is it that you wish to be alone? Maybe we can help."

Gruff said, "You are so full of yourself. How could you even begin to understand me? You're so young. You have no idea what I have been through in my life. You think you have all the answers?"

Spark said, "I don't have all the answers, but I am willing to listen and maybe help."

Gruff said, "You think you can help? Then you tell me—why did my child have to die? And why did my wife leave me? And for that matter, why were my own parents extremely cruel to me during my childhood?"

Spark said, "I am so sorry for your loss and your pain. There is no way for me to tell you why those things happened to you, and although I can't imagine your personal pain and frustration, I would be honored to share with you an explanation that has brought me comfort. Even though I am younger than you, I have also dealt with the painful and tragic loss of loved ones."

Gruff said, "Give me a break. There is no way you could have gone through what I have experienced."

Spark said, "You are right. Your experiences are your own, and I could never walk in your shoes. What I can do is share my experiences and what I have come to learn from them."

Gruff said, "Who cares what you have learned?"

Dawny said, "I do, so please continue."

Spark said, "One of the things I have learned is that the main purpose of our lives is to contribute to all there is by having many varied experiences. To further that purpose, we enter into agreements with other beings to participate in those experiences with us. These agreements are made at the higher-expanded-self level of consciousness."

Dawny asked, "Can you give an example of an agreement?"

"Sure. For example, one being may agree to be the abuser, and the other may agree to be the abused, in order for both souls to understand the experience. And after playing the part of abuser in one lifetime, that being might want to experience the opposite role of being abused in a different lifetime. Agreements are also made by the higher expanded self when a being enters and leaves this reality. Some of us may inhabit a body for a hundred years, and some may only be here for ten minutes or ten days. Nothing happens by chance or accident, and everything is purposefully designed."

Gruff said, "Now you are saying I agreed to be abused by my parents?"

"Well, actually, from the perspective of your nonphysical higher expanded self, yes. The perception of death or abuse or anything negative seems like a bad thing to the limited physical self because of the heavy illusion of duality here and the resulting pain and suffering

that follow. But to the higher expanded self, nothing is good or bad; each challenge is simply an agreement made out of love in order to assist in the expansion of consciousness and existence while we play for a short time in the world of physicality."

Dawny said, "It sounds like there is a part of us—which you have referred to as our higher expanded self—that knows more than what we are currently aware of."

Spark said, "I remember having wonderful conversations with my grandmother about this subject. I think I am beginning to understand that this current life we are living is not our only lifetime, and there is a reason we have lost the memories of our other lifetimes. However, the experiences in those lifetimes add to the collective body of knowledge contained within our higher expanded self."

Dawny, "So you're saying this isn't our only lifetime? Why would we choose to come back to experience all this pain and suffering?"

Gruff shouted, "There is no way I would choose the pain and suffering I have been through!"

Spark said, "I agree. However, that choice is not made on a conscious physical level; it is decided upon, and designed, at a much higher level of consciousness."

Dawny said, "What do you mean designed?"

Spark said, "Well, I am starting to understand what death is. Our consciousness is designed so that our eternal essence and spark continue to perpetually inhabit a different body when it is time to experience another set of experiences and challenges in the physical world. Death is simply a returning to our true selves. That's why my focus has started to change from being only consumed with my physical body to understanding that the body is the shell that houses the jewel within. That jewel is the immortal essence, or spark, or soul, that exists within each and every living thing. When a loved one dies, it is only the physical body that breaks down and disappears."

Dawny said, *"So when a loved one dies, only his or her physical body dies?"*

"Yes, our true self is immortal. We are not our bodies. The body is just a shell that houses the immortal spark within. We are even more alive when we are not in our physical bodies, because in that state, all fear is transmuted by the light and love of remembering the truth."

Dawny said, *"Wow! How are we more alive after we are no longer in our body?"*

"Because the only death is the death of the physical body. At that time, the body releases our true essence, and in that state of being, we are infinite, powerful, benevolent beings of pure energy. In that state of pure energy, before we decide to inhabit another physical body, there is a planning session with other immortal and infinite beings like ourselves. We talk, plan, and strategize about what we want to learn and experience in our next lives and what challenges we want to face so that we can overcome them. Ultimately, we learn from them and expand our knowledge of physical existence."

Dusky said, *"You're telling me that a part of me participated in the planning of all I have been through in my life?"*

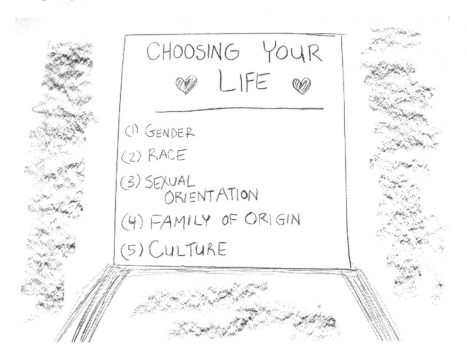

"Yes. From the perspective of our limited self, this is always going to be very difficult to comprehend. However, I have begun to understand that there is a part of our soul, our higher expanded self, that does not inhabit the physical body but exists in a higher dimension. When we are planning our other lives as physical beings, that piece of our soul that exists in a higher dimension is designing the plan while in a state of universal love, connectedness, truth, and wholeness."

Dawny asked, "Are we capable of experiencing a state of universal love, connectedness, truth, and wholeness while in our physical body?"

"Yes, we have the potential to, and many have experienced it. However, we designed our environment purposefully to block the truth in order to experience the duality of the game of life on earth. Therefore, most of the time, we experience conditional and unconditional love on earth, as opposed to universal love. But it is possible to allow the nonphysical, expanded part of ourselves to merge with the physical, *more limited aspect of ourselves, thereby creating an expanded state of being, while incarnate in a physical body."*

Gruff said, *"How come I have never felt connected?"*

"Because when we are in our physical bodies, there is a sense of separateness and isolation, as opposed to the state of total connection and knowledge that we are all one."

Dawny said, *"If we are all one, then what happens to me, Dawny, my personality?"*

Spark moved closer to Dawny and rubbed her legs against his in a gentle and loving manner. They both had strong feelings forming inside toward each other. Spark smiled at him. "Don't worry. Luckily, you will still be you. The paradox is that even though we experience this sensation of total connectedness with all of existence, we still retain our individuality, personality, and memories."

Dusky said, "Then why don't we remember we are all connected?"

"Because we purposefully have blocked our ability to understand the whole truth, in order to experience the many possibilities only available in an environment of duality and physicality."

Gruff interrupted. "Hey, if it is blocked, then how do you know what you know, and how are we able to even be talking about this if we are supposedly purposely blocked?"

Spark turned and looked at Gruff. "Well, what my grandmother explained to me is that the veil and blockage are diminishing to allow for greater numbers of us to experience and connect with our higher expanded selves. From this perspective, we view the physical lifetime more as a game that is an illusion. She explained that the truth is, **separateness is an illusion; we are never alone."**

Gruff, "If it is a game, then I don't want to play anymore. It sure doesn't feel like an illusion to me!"

Dusky said, "Yeah, I don't feel like this is very fun!"

Spark said, "That makes total sense because of the perspective you hold. The biggest lesson I am learning is that perspective is everything. It would be different if you were viewing your physical life from your higher expanded self. From that perspective, any pain, hardship, or strife that happens in the physical world is viewed as an opportunity to grow."

Gruff said, "So the purpose of this so-called game is to grow?"

"Yes, that is the purpose."

Dawny asked, "How do we grow?"

Spark said, "First, we need to know that learning and growing are optional. The first step is the desire and willingness to grow."

Dawny felt excited about his newfound love and her wisdom. "I have so much desire, and I am ready and willing. What is next?"

Spark beamed with the love she felt inside toward Dawny, which she saw reflected back to her from him. "Now that you are open and holding a perspective that is willing, this will allow the truth to surface. We grow through learning fundamental truths as we go through our life experiences. In any given situation, we need to be willing to ask ourselves, 'What is it that I am supposed to learn from this experience?' This allows your higher expanded self to provide the insight needed to grow and to navigate through physical creation, dense matter."

Gruff said, "The way you put it, it almost sounds like there is a reason and purpose for all of my pain. This is going to take some time for me to absorb. That's a big one! But what does dense matter have to do with anything?"

"It helps when you understand that your pain has a purpose and is not there needlessly. To answer your question, dense matter has to do with anything and everything in our physical world. It is a form of light and thought slowed down to such a degree that the vibrations of light begin to take physical form."

Gruff said, "I still don't understand. If the truth is that separateness is an illusion, and we are never alone, then why does this so-called illusion feel so real?"

Spark said, "It feels real because we are in a physical body in a physical world, and we have blocked our memory of our true essence. When we are creating and planning our other adventures in the physical world, we do not concern ourselves with creating a physical life that is easy. The purpose is to create and plan lives that lead to our ultimate expansion of wisdom."

Gruff said, "What kind of wisdom can come from sitting by my son while he takes his last breath and then being so devastated and unable to speak about my pain that my wife decides to leave me? Why would I choose this?"

Spark said, "I know it is very painful to grasp right now. If we could, for a moment, stop identifying with the pain and suffering and view those experiences from a more expanded perspective, and, Gruff, if you could for a moment imagine, almost as if we are watching a movie, it may start to make a bit of sense to you. We are all characters that agree out of love to play various parts or roles with a goal of being able to create a variety of experiences. Those experiences are delivered through a system of duality."

Gruff said, *"You're saying I've agreed out of love to experience the duality?"*

"Yes. All I know is that very often, I have learned my greatest lessons from my biggest challenges. I think that most of us learn effectively and grow from experiencing the negative sides of duality, such as pain, loss, fear, isolation, and lack of love and light. At other times, we learn effectively and grow from experiencing the positive sides of duality, such as love, joy, peace, balance, and connectedness. Both sides of duality act as teachers. There is no right or wrong, and from our nonphysical state of immortal infinity, we place zero judgment on whether we choose a lifetime of light or shadow, knowing we will have the opportunity to experience both."

Gruff said, *"Wait a minute. If there is no difference between what is right and what is wrong, then how do we know what is in our best interest if we are not supposed to use judgment?"*

"Instead of using judgment, what I do as an indicator of what is in my best interest is to use the more expansive perspectives of discernment, integrity, and intuition. What is right or wrong is determined by subjective beliefs and societal norms. Learning from the perspective of what is right and what is wrong is limiting and impacts our ability to see the whole picture."

Dawny said, *"Maybe you can give us an example of how discernment is used?"*

Spark said, *"Discernment may be used in many different ways. One useful way is looking at my past choices and experiences and asking myself, 'What have I learned from them? What blessings and gifts have I garnered from them?' Using discernment allows us to step aside from our current lives and ask ourselves questions that elicit the most appropriate outcomes, such as, 'What is the most loving choice? How will my choice create a win-win? What choice will lead to my highest good? What choice draws my focus? What choice evokes the most joy? Am I choosing out of love or fear?'"*

Dawny said, *"Like when we saw our sister changing, and we got scared. However, now with some insight, I can see that it is a good thing and not something to fear."*

Gruff said, *"If there is no judgment, what does it matter whether I choose to operate out of fear or love?"*

Spark said, *"There is no judgment, and it doesn't matter; however, in this closed environment of duality, the truth is, **love is the blueprint of creation; fear blocks our authentic power."***

Gruff said, *"If it doesn't matter, why is love, not fear, the blueprint of creation?"*

*"Because love is the vibration of the unified whole, and the energy vibration of love is a main ingredient in the act of establishing physical existence. My grandmother explained to me that the foundation of everything, when broken down to its original building blocks, reveals that love is at the core. She also said that fear is a manifestation of the illusion, and since the illusion is false, fear can simply be viewed as **f**alse **e**vidence **a**ppearing **r**eal. Fear is an absence of love and light that stems from the illusion of separation. Completely investing ourselves in the illusion of separation prevents us from realizing and accessing our authentic power."*

Dawny said, *"Gruff, when the horrific loss of your son happened and you continued to blame yourself and others, you separated from yourself, your family, and your community. You isolated and diminished your love and restricted your life by unconsciously repeating the patterns of anger and victimhood."*

Gruff said, *"So it is the emotion of fear that keeps me from accessing and experiencing my authentic power?"*

Spark said, *"Absolutely! The emotion of fear can create anger, shame, jealousy, resentment, guilt, envy, lack, self-judgment, blame, hatred, and illness. In the game of life, we get to play with love and fear and learn in a truly physical sense how wonderful love is by experiencing these opposites."*

Chapter 6 Highlights

**The antidote to any situation is to respond with love.

**The primary purpose of this reality is to assist in the ultimate expansion of creation by having many varied experiences.

**We enter into agreements with other divine sparks of creation to participate in those experiences together.

**We make these agreements at the higher-expanded-self level of consciousness and not while we are in a physical body.

**The higher expanded self also makes agreements regarding when a divine spark enters and leaves this reality.

**Nothing happens by chance or accident. We purposefully design everything.

**To the higher expanded self, nothing is good or bad, nor is there any judgment from our higher expanded self. Each challenge is simply an agreement made out of love.

**The current life we are living is not our only lifetime.

**Death is simply a returning to our true and authentic selves.

**Death of the physical releases our true essence, and in that state of being, we are immortal, infinite, and supremely powerful benign beings of pure energy.

**There is a part of our soul, our higher expand self, that does not inhabit the physical body. It exists in a higher dimension and is connected to us at all times.

**We designed the environment purposefully to block or veil the truth in order to experience the duality of the game of life on earth.

****The truth is, separateness is an illusion. We are never alone.**

**When you know that you are immortal and infinite, any pain, hardship, or strife that happens in the physical world is an opportunity to grow.

**The purpose is to create and plan lives that lead to our ultimate expansion of wisdom.

**We are characters that agree out of love to play various roles with the goal of creating a variety of experiences.

**Instead of using judgment as a measurement of what is in our best interest, a more expansive perspective is the use of discernment and intuition.

**Learning from the perspective of what is right and wrong impacts our ability to see the whole picture.

****The truth is, love is the blueprint of creation; fear blocks our authentic power.**

**The foundation of everything, when broken down to its original building blocks, reveals that love is at the core.

**Fear can simply be viewed as false evidence appearing real.

**Feeling the emotion of fear is the furthest a physical being can be from experiencing its higher expanded self.

7

Gruff said, "I understand now about what fear is; however, this is my reality, and I don't know any other way to live. Obviously, I have no clue who my higher expanded self is. What would be the benefit of me experiencing my higher expanded self?"

They all moved in closer as they noticed the energy around Gruff lighten up.

Spark said, "It is the closest we can come to feeling the utmost amount of joy and love in the physical world. The emotion of love is the closest a physical being can come to experiencing what it is like to be in our natural state. Gruff, can you think of a time when you experienced joy and love?"

Gruff said, "Not really."

"If you are willing, take a moment to think back to the birth of your son, and picture in your mind all of the sounds you heard and feelings you felt as you held him in your arms and looked into his eyes for the first time."

Gruff, with tears in his eyes, said, "Yes, I have experienced joy and love. But that was a long time ago, and I can't even imagine feeling that again in my life."

Spark said, "Well, you just experienced it now, and it brought you to tears. You know it is possible to feel the joy or love from a past experience, but to experience it in this now moment, you need to forgive."

"Forgive who?" Gruff asked.

"First yourself for how you have been treating yourself. Then others."

"What do I need to forgive myself for?"

Spark said, "You need to forgive yourself for holding yourself responsible for things beyond your understanding and control. You blame yourself and allow yourself to feel victimized, and the result is hiding out and isolating yourself from the world. You are internalizing all the guilt, anger, shame, and sorrow and keeping it bottled up and not allowing yourself to express and release those emotions. Those emotions eat away at you and cause illness and disease. That's why you need to forgive yourself in order to allow your healing process to begin."

Gruff said, "Well, what is the first step I need to take to begin to connect with my higher expanded self?"

"Forgiveness."

"How do I begin to forgive?"

Spark said, "First, you must have the desire to forgive. Second, you must have the willingness to accept responsibility for the role you played in creating the undesirable experience. Third, you must remember the truth that from an expanded perspective, all was designed out of love for the experience without judgment. Finally, you must stop the need to control an outcome. Also, *learn to trust that all is appropriate and ultimately leads to your spiritual evolution, even if the conscious mind can't see the whole picture."*

Gruff said, "Okay, so once I forgive myself and others, then what's next?"

"When you are able to forgive, that act of forgiveness allows the light to permeate the pain. The emotional charge from the memory is lifted. The present can change your perception of the past. Ultimately, there is no longer a need to remove your love and isolate yourself. The act of expressing compassion in forgiving oneself is the first step in connecting with your higher expanded self and leads to the ultimate truth that we are all connected and one."

Gruff said, "It's hard, though. I still don't understand how to forgive, because there is still so much pain and anger present when I think about the memory. How do I heal those painful emotions?"

Spark said, "Once you have embraced the truth that all is ultimately created out of love, have an understanding and acceptance of how this reality is purposefully designed, and have the intent to want to release the emotional charge, it is then within your responsibility to step into forgiveness and visualize the outcome you desire."

Gruff asked, "How do I begin to forgive myself and others?"

"Here is a very powerful, practical tool that I use every day in any situation, whether it is negative or positive. First, you visualize in your mind a pyramid of light."

"Does it matter what size the pyramid is?"

Spark said, "No, your pyramid may be any size or dimension that you desire. As you enter your pyramid of light, there is a large crystal chandelier hanging from the top, and radiating from it are spiraling rainbow-colored rays of light. The magnificent crystal chandelier is hanging over the center of a crystal table. As you move into the interior of the pyramid, look around: the walls and floor radiate soothing and healing inner light, and there are crystal chairs in a circle around the crystal table. When you lie on the table or place anything on it, the table automatically conforms perfectly around it. Under the table is a violet flame that is used to symbolically burn and neutralize the energies associated with the situation. In a negative *situation, for example, this is done in order to help transform and heal any negative energies around the situation."*

Gruff said, "The pain around the death of my son involves several people."

Spark said, "Yes, you would then call on the higher expanded selves of all who may have been involved and ask them to join you in your pyramid. You then place all the energy you have around this experience on the crystal table. Watch the violet flame from underneath blaze up and penetrate the energy you have placed on the table."

Gruff asked, "Is that all I need to do?"

"No. It must be clear that you are willing to let go of any negative feelings to allow the energy and the healing process to begin. Next, you want to begin to feel a release of your attachment to that energy so that it is neutralized."

Gruff said, "Okay, so once I feel the release of my emotions around it, what do I do?"

"After you feel the release, then visualize the crystal chandelier radiating streams of light like lightning hitting the table and infusing the neutralized energy, which was previously the negative, dark energy, with light."

Gruff said, "So is that it?"

"Well, since this is such a tragic situation, it will most likely take more than one time. You would repeat this mental process as often as you need until you no longer feel any negative emotions, such as guilt, shame, resentment, or blame, when thinking about it. If you are unable to visualize the process, it is just as effective to follow the steps of the process and allow yourself to feel the release."

Gruff began to heavily sob, and suddenly embarrassed, he lowered his head to hide his face and his uncontrollable tears. "I am sorry for crying."

Dawny said, "Oh no, there's nothing to apologize for. Crying is healthy. Although to some people vulnerability appears to be a sign of weakness, it is actually a sign of strength."

Gruff was surprised. "Strength?"

Dawny said, "Yeah, Gruff. The strength comes from having both the courage and the willingness to trust that everything is as it should be."

Gruff said, "I was taught that men shouldn't cry."

Dawny said, "We were all taught a lot of things that are not true and do not serve our best interests."

Spark said, "When we are healthy and balanced, we have combined both our masculine and feminine qualities."

Gruff became a bit defensive. "What do you mean? I have feminine qualities?"

Spark asked, "Well, have you ever felt any compassion, sensitivity, kindness, or tenderness toward another and the desire to nurture?"

Gruff said, "Of course. I felt all of those with my son."

Spark said, "Those characteristics are considered feminine qualities. Looking back, at that time, did you feel more balanced than you do now?"

"Yes, I guess, but as soon as my child got ill, I was thrown completely out of balance. Now, looking back, I see it was because I chose to stop showing kindness and compassion. I have tremendous guilt because I bullied so many people because of my fears and insecurities. I was taught to hurt people first before they have a *chance to hurt me. Now I realize that doing that hurts not only others but myself as well. How can I stop being a bully?"*

Spark said, "Since the first step is awareness and the desire to change, you have already begun the process by expressing your intent."

Dawny said, "Thinking about it, I know that I have to begin to practice forgiveness."

Spark said, "We all do. It is so important to forgive, and there are many tools to assist us. Personally, I use the pyramid tool because it is a powerful process that allows for a healing of emotional imbalance. Repeated use of the pyramid tool allows you to release all the guilt, shame, regret, and resentment you may have."

Gruff asked, "How often would I use the tools?"

Spark said, "Daily, and then as often as needed throughout the day. Maintaining balance is a moment-to-moment process, meaning that one has the potential to be in a state of balance or imbalance in any given moment."

Gruff asked, "How do I know when I am imbalanced?"

"A useful technique to determine this is to become one's own observer."

Dawny said, "How would I become my own observer?"

Spark said, "For me, there are a couple of tools that are useful in switching to operating as your own observer. First, you can pay attention to the repetitive thoughts in your head. Then you want to notice if there is a theme to your self-talk. For example, are you being a judge, critic, or victim? Next, label the voice as the judge or the victim. Each time you notice and label it, you are operating as the observer."

Dawny said, *"What is the benefit of becoming my own observer and learning to maintain balance?"*

"When you are balanced, you no longer attract drama and chaos. Like attracts like; therefore, you attract to yourself a reflection of that balance. Eventually, balance leads to a profound feeling of being one with all, and the duality illusion is diminished."

Dusky said, *"I want to diminish the illusion of duality. So is labeling your repetitive thoughts the only way to become your own observer and feel connected as one?"*

Spark said, *"No, there are many ways. Another technique I have used is to imagine a part of yourself floating up to the ceiling and looking down on the physical portion of you that is engaged in the negative self-talk. From this elevated position, you are now the observer."*

Chapter 7 Highlights

**The emotion of love is the closest a physical being can come to experiencing what it is like to be in our natural state.

**It is possible to feel the joy or love from a past experience, but to experience it in this now moment, you need to begin to forgive.

**When you are able to forgive, that act of forgiveness allows the light to permeate the pain.

**The steps to connect with your higher expanded self are the following:

(1) forgiving yourself and others

(2) taking personal responsibility

(3) accepting that everything is designed out of love

(4) surrendering the need to control the outcome

**Using the pyramid of light is a powerful, practical tool.

**Although vulnerability appears to most people to be a sign of weakness, it is actually a sign of strength.

**Strength comes from having the courage and the willingness to trust that everything is as it should be.

**Maintaining balance is a moment-to-moment process.

**When we are healthy and balanced, we have integrated within us both our masculine and feminine qualities.

**A useful tool for becoming the observer includes the following:

(1) Pay attention to the repetitive thoughts in your head.

(2) Identify the theme of your self-talk.

(3) Label it.

**A second tool is visualization. See yourself floating up to the ceiling and looking down on the physical portion of you that is engaged in the negative self-talk.

**Becoming the observer allows a greater perspective, which leads to balance.

**When you are balanced, you are no longer attracting to yourself the energy of drama and chaos. Because like attracts like, you attract to yourself a reflection of that balance.

8

Dawny said, "You keep mentioning that we are connected to the oneness. I still don't understand. What do you mean we are all connected and are all one? Would you give me an example?"

Spark said, "I'd be happy to. Imagine in your mind a huge, all-powerful ball of divine energy. This energy consists of and fills up every space, meaning nothing exists outside this ball of energy."

Dusky said, "So everything in the universe is inside this ball of energy?"

"Yes, everything in existence is inside this ball of energy. The ball consists of everything everywhere and is completely unified."

Gruff asked, "When was this divine ball of energy created?"

"This ball of energy was never created. It has always existed. It has no beginning and no end. It is outside of time and the illusion of linear time. Standardized, linear time as we know it is an illusion. When we are operating from a third-dimension consciousness, time is linear, meaning it is viewed as a line from past events to present and then future events."

Dusky said, *"If linear time is an illusion, then what's the purpose of linear time?"*

"If you can, think of it this way: the process of slowing down the light over time, meaning the time it takes for something to appear in our physical reality, allows the individual to observe the process of creation. That said, the purpose of linear time is to allow the experience of creation to be witnessed and felt by us all."

Dusky asked, *"Is that why our sister kept saying it is about the journey, not the destination?"*

Spark said, *"Actually, I like that saying. It sounds like your sister was starting to realize that being present, and experiencing the present moment, holds more meaning than simply rushing through life in an attempt to accomplish goals. That's why being present in every given moment is such a significant part of experiencing the physical world."*

Dawny asked, "What does all of that have to do with whether you and I are connected and are all one?"

Spark said, "Let's see if I can explain it further. Imagine that this all-powerful divine energy has a consciousness and is aware of itself. As it is a completely unified energy, it is not possible for it to separate from itself."

Dawny said, "So everywhere it looks, it sees itself, and everywhere it moves, it finds itself?"

"Exactly. Then imagine that this loving energy wants to experience the sensation of sending love to itself and receiving love back from itself."

Dawny said, "Why would this energy want to do that? For that matter, how would it?"

"Because the concept of giving and receiving implies separateness, and the unified whole is simply whole. Therefore, it wanted to experience itself in a new and different way. The energy ball, being all-powerful, engages in a fiction. Knowing that it is an infinite energy with the potential to grow and expand infinitely and in all directions, it creates the illusion of separateness."

Dawny said, "How does it do that?"

"Knowing that it can never really be separate from itself, the divine energy engages in the illusion of separateness by dividing itself up into smaller bits and pieces of energy. Each bit and piece of energy spark is given the ability of free will to further divide itself up into smaller pieces of energy."

Dawny said, "Are you saying that every spark has free will?"

Spark said, "Yes, my grandmother said that every spark in our world has free will and is given the ability by using light to create. Universes are created as light is slowed down and formed into dense matter."

Dawny said, "Okay, I am getting a bit dizzy. Is there any way you can give us a tangible example?"

At that moment, it began to drizzle, and across the tops of the trees, a beautiful rainbow appeared.

Spark said, *"How perfect! See that beautiful rainbow up there?"*

They all stopped to look. Spark continued. *"That rainbow is made of light that is vibrating much faster than the forest that surrounds us. If the light of that rainbow was slowed down in vibration and specific patterns and geometric shapes were formed, then the energy of that light could be shaped into physical matter. Everything in creation consists of light vibrating at different speeds and frequencies."*

Dusky asked, *"Are we made of light?"*

"Yes, every cell in our body contains light. The physical body is an example of light that is vibrating at a slower rate than nonphysical reality, and the body acts as a vehicle in order to engage in physical

reality. The spark of light is who we truly are, and that spark is always connected to the whole, because everything is ultimately one."

Dawny said, "When the sparks continue to divide and engage in separation, do they move further away from the original energy?"

Spark said, "No, what I have been told, and now am beginning to understand, is that the distance is only an illusion, because there can never truly be any separation from the whole. This is the true connectivity of all living things. What is so amazing is that inside each of us is a spark of the all-powerful divine energy of the unified whole."

Dawny said, "So you're suggesting that each of us is a spark of this energetic whole?"

"Absolutely. Just because a spark chooses to explore the physical dimension by placing a portion of itself in a physical body does not mean it is separated from the unified whole. Also, each spark contains within it the exact makeup and details of the unified whole."

Gruff said, "Let me see if I understand what you're saying. If a spark of this energy ball were scooped up and examined, the contents would be the same energy it was taken from?"

Spark said, "Yes. My grandmother explained that there is no permanent separation, just as there can be no destruction of any part of the whole. Not only that, but each spark of this whole is so entangled with the unified whole that it stays connected no matter how far it travels."

Dawny said, "Maybe you can give us an example, because this idea is a bit complicated."

"Sure. Imagine you are a drop of water in a vast, beautiful ocean. As water, you are able to travel freely wherever you choose, because you are connected to every other drop of water in the vast ocean. Now imagine that you are scooped up into a glass. Inside this glass, you still possess the same attributes and characteristics of the water you are, yet your movement is restricted due to the glass container. Inside this glass, you might feel like you are separate from all the other water in the world, but the feeling of separation is only due to the fact that a physical shell is now containing you.

"Once you are poured back into the ocean, you reunite with the rest of the ocean, and once again, you are the whole ocean, but with the added experience of what it feels like to be restricted and separate due to your time enclosed within the glass. Once you reunite with the ocean, you retain your memories, personality, and *characteristics you've always had, yet at the same time, you are also the whole ocean and completely unified and one with all.*

"The physical body is just like the glass. It simply houses our true essence. Sometimes it may feel like we are separate from every other thing living in these bodies, but once the body is gone, we return to the oneness and unity of our true essence."

Dawny asked, "Why does a divine spark choose to experience separation from the whole?"

Spark said, "Keep in mind that there can be no actual separation from the whole, only an illusion of separation. Knowing that there is no actual separation, as divine sparks, we get the opportunity to play the game of hide-and-seek by forgetting our true connection to the unified whole while at the same time seeking it. With this veil over our memory, we are free to experience the lessons of duality by experiencing both the positives and negatives of life on earth. All experiences, as well as the knowledge and wisdom learned from those lessons, are added to the total expansion and essence of the unified whole."

Gruff said, "Tell me again why we choose to experience bad things."

Spark said, "Gruff, I know your experience was really painful, but remember what we have been talking about. Since it is only an illusion, no experience is judged as either positive or negative or bad or good. As divine sparks, we choose to temporarily feel separate from the whole because in doing so, we help the expansion of ourselves through our own growth and, ultimately, the expansion of the unified whole."

Dusky asked, "Is that why bad things happen to good people and bad people?"

"Exactly!"

Gruff said, "So again, what you are saying is that we get to play with the full spectrum of emotions?"

"Exactly. In this game of life, we get to play with love and fear and learn in a truly physical sense how wonderful love is by experiencing its opposite. It is up to us to figure out which emotions feel the best and which ones lead to our ultimate realization and truth. Although this physical life is an illusion of separation, eventually, we all remember we are one."

Dawny said, "So if I am a spark of the original unified energy, are there other parts of my energy also engaging in the illusion of separation?"

"Yes, the goal is to expand oneness by exercising free will and having as many varied experiences as possible. Each spark divides itself up into many smaller pieces of energy, and those sparks then have many simultaneously concurrent experiences in physicality."

Gruff said, "So why do we have births and deaths?"

"Metaphorically speaking, birth and death are the mechanisms that allow us to try on many sets of clothes. The energy that is the unified whole, and the sparks of that whole, has always existed and will forever exist. Birth and death are words we use to describe a process of transitioning, in which the soul enters and exits the physical world. The process is all a part of our growth. Death allows us to free ourselves from the physical body of one lifetime and take on a different body, thus providing each spark the experience of extreme diversity. Similar to the third dimension, for example, there may exist many different versions of yourself, all existing in slightly different vibrations or frequencies simultaneously."

Gruff said, "Simultaneously? Now you've lost me. How is that possible?"

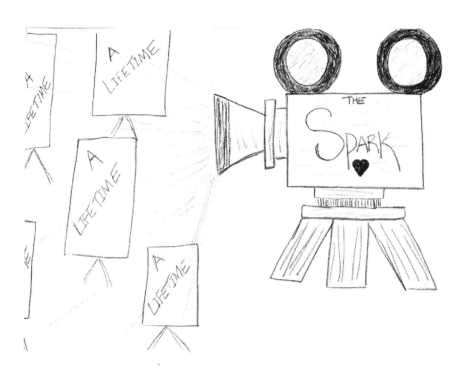

Spark said, "Imagine one grand central projector, and this projector has the ability to project its light onto all the various screens at a theater simultaneously. The grand projector represents our multidimensional higher expanded self, and each screen represents a different lifetime. All these lifetimes are happening simultaneously, unaware of the others' existence."

Gruff said, "Why is it that we are not aware of the other simultaneous lifetimes?"

"Because each version of us is solely focused upon participating in the current lifetime it finds itself in. As we integrate and expand in consciousness, all of the memories and lessons we learned from our experiences are remembered in our higher state of consciousness.

Also, as we progress in understanding and move to higher realms of consciousness, we get to play with different challenges."

Dusky asked, "Do all sparks participate in the physical world?"

"No. I have been told that in some dimensions, there are nonphysical beings that are just vibrating light, and no dense matter is present. In many of these dimensions, the game plan is the same—to add to the whole by exercising free will."

Dawny said, "Sometimes I get chills or shivers all over my body, and it feels like there is the presence of someone or something around. Is that because they are in another dimension and I can't see them? I am trying to understand what you mean by dimension."

"It's possible. However, getting chills or shivers can represent a number of things. Let me see if I can explain what a dimension is. It is comprised of frequencies and wavelengths of light that are accessible to levels of consciousness. These wavelengths of light have attributes associated with greater levels of awareness. As each spark continues to expand in consciousness and shift from a limited perspective of duality and a consciousness of separation to a perspective of unity, it moves closer in vibration toward reuniting with the one unified whole."

Dusky said, "So you are saying that no matter how awful I am, I won't be excluded?"

"Of course not. One thing I know to be true is that the unified whole neither judges nor favors any part of itself over any other part. This is because it is impossible for a unified whole to point out one part of itself and express a preference since in unity, there cannot be separation. It is one. It neither approves nor disapproves of itself or the actions of its temporarily illusory fragments of itself."

Dusky said, "So we are temporarily illusory fragments of the unified whole?"

"Yes!"

Gruff said, "So all of us agreed out of love to participate in the game of life on earth by immersing ourselves in duality?"

"Yes!"

Dawny said, "We are only pretending to be separate, when in truth, we are all one and never alone?"

"Yes!"

Dusky said, "All we have to do to experience our true power is to come from love by thinking with our hearts instead of acting out of fear?"

Spark said, "Yes! And always remember that the key to opening oneself up to one's higher expanded self is remaining in a state of appreciation and expressing gratitude for oneself and all living things."

Gruff scratched his head. "Well, young one, you have sure given me a lot to think about."

Dusky said, "I will never think the same way again."

Dawny said, "Thank you so much, Spark, for sharing your wisdom and love."

Chapter 8 Highlights

**Time is an illusion of the physical world.

**The purpose of time is to allow the experience of manifestation to be witnessed and felt by us all.

**The process of slowing down the light over time, meaning the time it takes for something to appear in one's physical reality, is to allow the individual to observe the process of creation.

**Being present in every given moment is a significant part of experiencing the physical world.

**In the nonphysical, there is no time lag between thought and manifestation.

**Everything in creation consists of light vibrating at different speeds and frequencies.

**Every cell in our bodies contains the essence of light from the unified whole.

**There can be no permanent separation from the unified whole, just as there can be no destruction of any part of the unified whole.

**Our life on earth is like a game of hide-and-seek. Our true essence is purposefully hidden by a veil placed over our memory, and our goal is to seek and find it within.

**Duality is the system in which we play the game of hide-and-seek.

**In the game of life, we get to play with love and fear and learn in a truly physical sense how wonderful love is by experiencing its opposite.

**Physical life is an illusion of separation, and eventually, we all return to the awareness of oneness.

**Birth and death are made-up concepts used to assist us as we learn and play in the physical world.

**We have always existed and shall continue to exist forever.

**As we move from one density of consciousness and dimension to the next in the illusion of separation, all of the memories and lessons we learned from our experiences are remembered in our higher states of consciousness.

**There are dimensions that consist of physical beings both similar to and dissimilar from us. In many of these dimensions, the game plan is the same—to add to the whole by exercising free will.

**A dimension is comprised of frequencies and wavelengths that are accessible to levels of consciousness.

**Our judgments from our limited selves create separation. However, it is impossible for a unified whole to point out one part of itself and express a preference, because in unity, there cannot be separation. That's why there is no judgment upon death.

**We are only pretending to be separate, when in truth, we are all one and never alone.

**The key to opening oneself up to one's higher expanded self is remaining in a state of appreciation and expressing gratitude for oneself and all living things.

9

As night fell, exhausted from all they had learned, they all bid each other a good night and departed for the evening.

As dawn broke the next morning, Spark slowly emerged from her cocoon. With each labored movement, as Spark shook off the remnants of her outer shell, she realized that the forest was empty. Dusky, Dawny, Gruff, and Omni were nowhere to be seen, and as the realization set in, Spark cracked a smile. She thought, It was all a dream.

All of the characters she'd met in the forest, and even the storm, had been simply teaching tools to aid in her awakening. Dusky, Dawny, and Gruff had never existed, but she'd learned much from the experiences she'd assimilated as she imagined each of them. Each truth had become another layer of her cocoon, and as she'd allowed herself to go deeper and deeper into her inner space, her own higher expanded self had introduced more and more catalysts to allow Spark to go even deeper. Ultimately, Spark realized that perhaps nothing really existed except for love and the inner thoughts, attitudes, and feelings that resonated within her.

Even though the forest critters she'd imagined were only illusory, she knew their attributes were all contained within her. She was grateful for their presence in helping her awaken and for her own ability to create such fantastic and imaginative creations to further aid in her own spiritual enfoldment. As the reality of her inner journey continued to amaze and astound Spark, she pondered the realization that she'd created the whole story and all the characters. She quickly realized that she was no longer the caterpillar she once had been. With one final push and an inhalation and exhalation of breath, Spark freed herself from her cocoon completely, and without looking back, she spread her wings and took flight.

The Seven Truths

I.   If you always go within, you will never go without. Abundance is within.

II.   Separateness is an illusion, we are never alone.

III. We are eternal and are all one.

IV.   Thinking with our hearts and feeling with our heads allows for balance.

V.   You create your reality; your outer world is a reflection of your inner world.

VI.   Love is the blueprint of creation; fear blocks our authentic power.

VII. Duality provides the opportunity to grow, and expressing gratitude enhances that growth.

Beth Fortman-Brand's Biography

Beth Fortman-Brand is an intuitive strategist (IS) for personal and corporate clients worldwide. For almost twenty-five years, Beth has designed and conducted numerous workshops and seminars in public and corporate arenas. The purpose of these workshops is to teach people how to develop and successfully apply a variety of skills required for building and maintaining healthy relationships both personally and professionally. Not only is Beth engaging, dynamic, and witty, but she also is an expert in the how-tos of living a successful lifestyle and creating healthy relationships.

Beth's medium-like intuition provides her with the ability to see the truth in anybody's story, thereby expediting the healing process. Beth is highly skilled in assisting others in learning to think, feel, and act from their hearts instead of their heads. Beth's innate ability to tap into and hear individuals' higher selves guides them to consciously choose to come from love rather than fear, thereby allowing the unlimited possibilities of their higher intuitive selves to be realized.

Beth received her bachelor of science degree in sociology from UCLA in 1986 with an emphasis on social programs, social policies, and psychology. She has studied and taught behavioral science and the dynamics of personal relationships extensively for the past thirty years.

Since 1986, Beth has been a successful financial consultant and business owner. Beth was recognized in *Who's Who in Top Female Executives* in 1989. From 1979 through 1986, Beth taught cooperation workshops for teachers while teaching students at the secondary level for the Los Angeles Unified School District.

Beth is an extraordinary communicator. She has a natural ability to connect with individuals and groups of all ages and diverse backgrounds. Therefore, Beth is able to teach anyone who is willing how to have successful, loving relationships.

Beth's highly intuitive skills, intriguing career, and life transitions have led her to share her transformational experiences for the benefit of others. Beth's book *The Power of Love: Living from Our Hearts* (currently available in more than twenty-five thousand bookstores) provides effective tools and valuable information for transformation, teaching how to experience a life filled with amazing love, total peace, and great joy.

Since 1995, Beth has been a consultant and adviser to life coaches, attorneys, financial consultants, and personnel (including top executives) of major insurance companies, such as AIG, Allstate, Aviva, Travelers, Safeco, GE Capital, CNA, and Pacific Life. She is credited for being instrumental in the success of Medivest Benefit Advisors. Beth coaches and advises executives in the movie and television industry nationally as well. Beth is also the executive producer of Power of Love Productions and CEO of http://www.blessourchildren.org, an online store that assists children's charities. Beth has appeared in, cowritten, and coproduced more than twenty spiritually inspiring self-help videos and a documentary called *Love*, which addresses the legalization of same-sex marriage. She has also been working on projects that provide a bridge between the mainstream community and the LGBTQ community through the creation of antibullying and inspirational videos. Beth has cowritten a screenplay called *Power of Love* and is currently working on the preproduction process. Beth lives in Wood Ranch, California, with her loving husband, Doug Brand.

Matthew Schonbrun's Biography

For the past fifteen years, Matthew Schonbrun has worked as a criminal prosecutor in Los Angeles, and he was a former candidate for superior court judge. He holds a juris doctorate degree, a bachelor of arts degree in sociology, and a practitioner's license in neurolinguistic programming and is a certified Reiki practitioner. He is a frequent guest speaker at law enforcement seminars and bar association meetings relating to criminal prosecution methods, trains new attorneys in trial skills and oral advocacy, and is the published author of several legal as well as metaphysical articles.

He has spent much of his life actively engaged in the process of seeking answers to fundamental questions concerning our perception of reality and the world we live in. Matthew is committed to being a conscious creator of his experiences by allowing the divine within to be the architect of his life, and strives to continue to awaken to the knowing that his divinity is incarnate. By remembering that we are all one being, Matthew adopts a nonjudgmental perspective, which allows him to have a more expanded and connected view of the world. He lives in Los Angeles with his wife, Jacky; son, Liam; and daughter, Skye.

Agnes Deason's Biography

For more than twenty-five years, Agnes Deason has been a personal relationship coach. She has built a successful international practice in personal development and relationship skills. Agnes has designed and provides effective foundational tools that increase an individual's levels of creativity and sense of purpose.

As a student and teacher of life and love, she devotes her time and energy to helping others find their true understanding of self. Agnes continues to learn about love as energy and the ways to use her inner sight to identify people's core issues and themes. She has a remarkable ability to find ways to guide and assist others in healing themselves. Agnes teaches her clients how to bring balance into all aspects of their lives. She delights in encouraging people to bring divine love into everyday living. As a result of the individual work she provides, her clients' quality of relationships with themselves and others improves dramatically. Most importantly, her clients experience a tremendous increase in self-acceptance and self-love.

Agnes lives with her husband in Wood Ranch, California.

Printed in the United States
By Bookmasters